Microsoft®
Windows 7
for the Over 50s

Prentice Hall
is an imprint of

Harlow, England • London • New York • Boston • San Francisco • Toronto • Sydney • Singapore • Hong Kong
Tokyo • Seoul • Taipei • New Delhi • Cape Town • Madrid • Mexico City • Amsterdam • Munich • Paris • Milan

PEARSON EDUCATION LIMITED

Edinburgh Gate
Harlow CM20 2JE
Tel: +44 (0)1279 623623
Fax: +44 (0)1279 431059
Website: www.pearsoned.co.uk

First published in Great Britain in 2010

ISBN: 978-0-273-72918-1

British Library Cataloguing-in-Publication Data
A catalogue record for this book is available from the British Library

Library of Congress Cataloging-in-Publication Data
Ballew, Joli.
  Microsoft Windows 7 for the over 50s : in simple steps / Joli Ballew.
     p. cm.
  ISBN 978-0-273-72918-1 (pbk.)
  1. Microsoft Windows (Computer file) 2. Operating systems (Computers) I. Title.
  QA76.76.O63B35927 2010
  005.4′46--dc22
                    2009036763

10 9 8 7 6 5 4 3 2 1
13 12 11 10 09

Designed by pentacorbig, High Wycombe
Typeset in 11/14 pt ITC Stone Sans by 3
Printed by Ashford Colour Press Ltd., Gosport, UK

The publisher's policy is to use paper manufactured from sustainable forests.

Microsoft®

Windows 7
for the Over 50s

in Simple steps

Joli Ballew

Use your computer with confidence

Get to grips with practical computing tasks with minimal time, fuss and bother.

In Simple Steps guides guarantee immediate results. They tell you everything you need to know on a specific application; from the most essential tasks to master, to every activity you'll want to accomplish, through to solving the most common problems you'll encounter.

Helpful features

To build your confidence and help you to get the most out of your computer, practical hints, tips and shortcuts feature on every page:

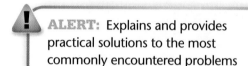 **ALERT:** Explains and provides practical solutions to the most commonly encountered problems

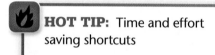 **HOT TIP:** Time and effort saving shortcuts

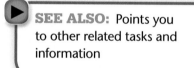 **SEE ALSO:** Points you to other related tasks and information

 **DID YOU KNOW?** Additional features to explore

WHAT DOES THIS MEAN?

Jargon and technical terms explained in plain English

Practical. Simple. Fast.

Dedication:

For Mom, I miss you deeply.

Author's acknowledgements:

The older I get and the more books I write, the more people there are to thank and acknowledge. I am thankful for many things, including the opportunities offered by Pearson Education every time there's a new Windows edition, and the awesome team of editors and typesetters who work tirelessly to turn my words into pages and those pages into books.

I am thankful that I have a supportive family, including Jennifer, Andrew, Dad and Cosmo. I am thankful to my extended family for all playing a role in my daughter's upbringing and success. I am thankful for my health, much to the credit of my doctor, Kyle Molen. Between the lot of them, they keep me in check, on track, healthy and sometimes even sound.

I miss my mother, who passed away in February 2009, but I am thankful that some day I'll be able to see and talk to her again, something she worked hard to make me understand shortly after she passed away.

And finally, I'm thankful to my agent, Neil Salkind, who encourages me, is my biggest fan and who always has my back, no matter what. Everyone should have someone like that in their lives.

Contents at a glance

**Top 10 Windows 7
Problems Solved**

Contents

7 Windows Media Center

8 Getting online

9 Working with email

10 Stay secure

11 Working with files and folders

12 Change system defaults

13 Create a HomeGroup, and share data and printers

14 Fix problems

Top 10 Windows 7 Problems Solved

Top 10 Windows 7 Tips

Tip 1: Open your personal folder and its subfolders

You store the data you want to keep in your personal folder. Your data includes documents, pictures, music, contacts, videos, and more. The Start menu offers a place to access this folder easily, as well as installed programs, Windows 7 features and applications (like the Calculator, Notepad and Internet Explorer), recent items you've accessed and Games, among other things.

1 Click Start.

2 Click your user name.

3 View the items in your personal folder.

> 🔥 **HOT TIP:** Double-click any folder inside your personal folder to open it. Click the back arrow to return to the previous view (also called a window).

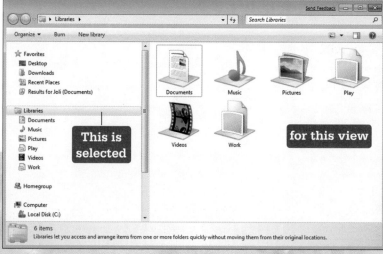

> ⚠️ **ALERT:** Notice in the screenshot how Libraries is selected in the left (Navigation) pane. If you have another folder selected, your screen won't look like this.

Most folders that you will open will have other folders inside them. These are called subfolders. You open a subfolder in the same way as a main folder, by double-clicking. Since you'll be going 'deeper' into the folder when you do this, you'll want to click the 'Back' button to work your way back out.

4 Click Start, and click your name in the Start menu. This opens your personal folder.

5 Double-click any subfolder to open it. Here, I've clicked Favorites in the Navigation pane, and selected Contacts to view the contacts listed on my computer.

6 Click the Back button to return to your personal folder.

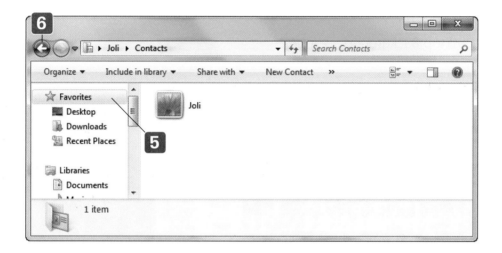

 HOT TIP: Note the Search area just underneath the red X in the top right corner of the window. You can type anything there to search for it in the present window.

? **DID YOU KNOW?**
You can also right-click any folder and choose Open. Right-clicking opens the 'contextual' menu, a hidden menu with exceptionally useful options.

 DID YOU KNOW?
You can click on anything you see in the Start menu to open it, and then close it using the X in the top right corner of the program window. Don't worry – you can't hurt anything!

Tip 2: Configure a rotating background with your favourite pictures

You can configure the desktop background to change automatically. The time intervals you can select range from every 10 seconds to once a day. You can use the pictures that come with Windows 7 or you can choose a folder of your own. You might want to create a folder that contains pictures of your family, and use that as your background.

1 Right-click an empty area of the desktop and click Personalize.

2 Click Desktop Background.

HOT TIP: You can configure a rotating background using the pictures in the Windows Desktop Backgrounds picture location. With that location selected, click Select all and choose how often to change the picture.

3 To choose a folder that contains pictures you've added, click Browse, and locate the folder to use, then click Select all and choose how often to change the picture.

4 Click Save changes.

Tip 3: Write a letter with Notepad

If you need to create and print a simple document like a grocery or to-do list, or need to put together a weekly newsletter that you send via email, there's no reason to purchase a large office suite like Microsoft Office (and learn how to use it) when Notepad will do just fine. Although you can't create and insert tables, add endnotes, add text boxes or perform similar tasks with Notepad, you may never need to anyway.

1 Click Start.

2 In the Start Search window, type Notepad.

3 Click Notepad under Programs. (Note that you may see other results, as shown here.)

4 Click once inside Notepad, and start typing.

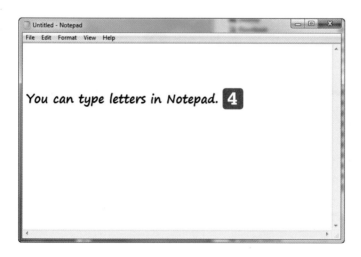

? DID YOU KNOW?
The Format menu includes options for setting the font, font style, font size, and more.

! ALERT: If you close Notepad before saving the file, your work will be lost!

Tip 4: Install a printer or scanner

Printer installation is almost always a straightforward affair. You connect the device to the PC, plug it in, turn it on and wait while the driver installs automatically. Windows 7 has a vast library of drivers and if it can't find what it needs, it'll check for the driver online.

1 Connect the printer to a wall outlet.

2 Connect the printer to the PC using either a USB cable or a parallel port cable.

3 Insert the CD for the device, if you have it. However, if a pop-up message appears regarding the CD, click the X to close the window.

4 Turn on the device.

5 Wait while the driver is installed.

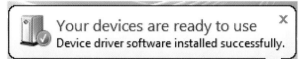

 DID YOU KNOW?
The reason you should let Windows 7 install a device on its own is because when you install a CD that comes with a device, you'll probably also install applications you'll never use and don't need.

? **DID YOU KNOW?**
Leave the CD in the drive. If Windows 7 wants to access information on the CD, it will acquire it from there.

🔥 **HOT TIP:** If, after using the printer a few times, you need to access advanced printer preferences like printing in reverse or applying light or heavy ink, insert the printer CD again and install only the printer software (and nothing else).

Tip 5: Download and install Windows Live Essentials

You have to download and install Windows Live applications, and you really should get them. Windows 7 does not come with an email program, a photo-editing program or a Movie Maker program. Windows Live Essentials has all of this and more. The suite of programs is available on the Internet. If you've never downloaded and/ or installed a program before, you may be a little nervous about doing so. Don't worry, it's really easy, safe and secure, and Microsoft has set it up so that the process requires very little input from you. There are only a few steps: go to the website, click the Download link, and wait for the download and installation process to complete.

1 Open Internet Explorer and go to http://www.windowslive.com/.

2 Look for the Download now button and click it. You'll be prompted to click Download now once more on the next screen.

3 Click Run, and when prompted, click Yes.

4 When prompted, select the items to download. If the programs have already been installed by the computer manufacturer, you'll be informed what programs were installed and what is still available.

5 When prompted to select your settings, make the desired choices. You can't go wrong here; there are no bad options.

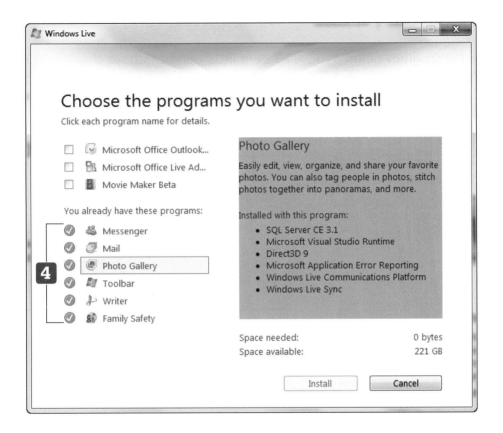

? DID YOU KNOW?

It's OK to select all of these programs if you think you'll use them; they are all free. However, Family Safety can get a tad annoying, so only install that if you have children who will use your computer.

🔥 HOT TIP: During this installation process, go ahead and download Mail, Messenger, and Toolbar; you'll find all three useful.

Tip 6: Get a Windows Live account

When you use 'Live' services, like Windows Live Photo Gallery, you log into them using a free, Windows Live account. You need a Windows Live account which provides an email address and password you use to log on to your Live programs on the Internet.

1 If you do not already have a Windows Live account, click Sign up after the installation of Live Mail completes. (You can also go to http://signup.live.com.)

2 Fill out the required information and click I accept when finished.

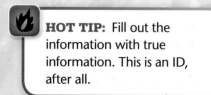

DID YOU KNOW?

You can use your Windows Live email account as a regular email address, or simply use it to log into Live services on the Internet.

HOT TIP: Fill out the information with true information. This is an ID, after all.

Tip 7: Watch, pause and rewind live TV

When you open Media Center, TV is the default option, and Recorded TV is selected. To watch live television, you'll need to use the mouse, keyboard or remote control to move to the right, to live TV. While watching live TV, you can watch, pause and rewind the show you're watching (and fast-forward through previously paused programming).

1 Open Media Center.

2 Move to the right of recorded TV and click live tv.

3 Position the mouse at the bottom of the live TV screen to show the controls.

4 Use the controls to manage live TV.

ALERT: It's not possible to fast forward live TV; you have to have paused some live TV first.

ALERT: If you receive an error when you click live tv, it's either because you do not have the television signal properly set up or you don't have a TV tuner.

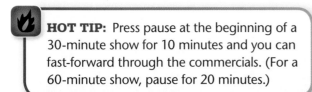

Record   Channel down   Stop   Play/ pause   Mute   Volume up

Channel up   Rewind   Fast forward   Volume down

HOT TIP: Press pause at the beginning of a 30-minute show for 10 minutes and you can fast-forward through the commercials. (For a 60-minute show, pause for 20 minutes.)

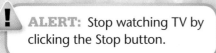

ALERT: Stop watching TV by clicking the Stop button.

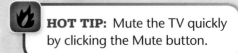

HOT TIP: Mute the TV quickly by clicking the Mute button.

Tip 8: Attach a picture to an email using a right-click

You can create an email that contains an attachment by right-clicking the file you want to attach. This method attaches the files to a new email, which is fine if you want to create a new email. The only problem with this is that it doesn't work if you'd rather send forwards or replies. However, this method has a feature other methods don't. With it, you can resize any images you've selected before sending them. This is a great perk because many pictures are too large to send via email, and resizing them helps manage an email's size.

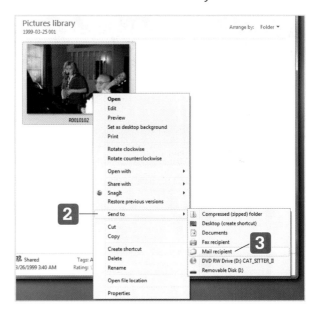

1 Locate the file you'd like to attach and right-click it.

2 Point to Send to.

3 Click Mail recipient.

4 If the item you're attaching is a picture, choose the picture size.

5 If prompted to send a photo email, click Yes. You'll be able to edit the picture in the email and users can view multiple pictures as a slide show.

? DID YOU KNOW?

800 × 600 is usually the best option when sending pictures via email.

? DID YOU KNOW?

You can email from within applications, such as Microsoft Word or Excel. Generally, you'll find the desired option under the File menu, as a submenu of Send.

! ALERT: Avoid sending large attachments, especially to people you know have a dial-up modem or those who get email only on a small device like a BlackBerry, iPhone or Mobile PC.

Tip 9: Add a new user account

You created your user account when you first turned on your new Windows 7 PC. Your user account is what defines your personal folders as well as your settings for desktop background, screen saver, and other items. You are the 'administrator' of your computer, even if your user name is Grandma or Dad. If you share the PC with someone, they should have their own user account too.

1 Click Start.

2 Click Control Panel.

3 Click Add or remove user accounts.

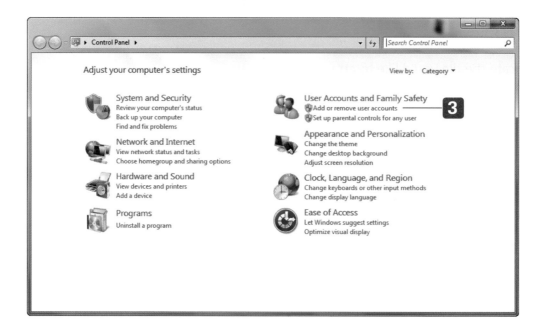

ALERT: If every person who accesses your PC has their own standard user account and password, and if every person logs on using that account and then logs off the PC each time they've finished using it, you'll never have to worry about anyone accessing anyone else's personal data.

ALERT: All accounts should have a password applied to them. You can do that by clicking the user name and opting to apply a password.

4 Click Create a new account.

5 Type a new account name, verify Standard user is selected, and click Create Account.

Tip 10: Use System Restore

System Restore regularly creates and saves *restore points* that contain information about your computer that Windows uses to work properly. If your computer starts acting oddly, you can use System Restore to restore your computer to a time when the computer was working properly.

1 Open System Restore.

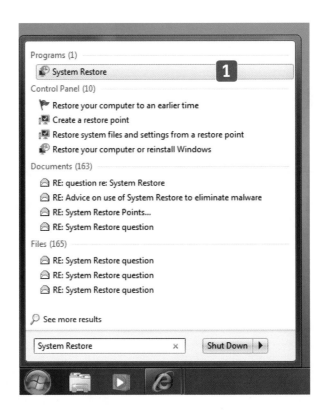

! ALERT: System Restore can't be enabled unless the computer has at least 300 MB of free space on the hard disk, or if the disk is smaller than 1 GB.

? DID YOU KNOW?
Because System Restore works only with its own system files, running System Restore will not affect any of your personal data. Your pictures, email, documents, music, etc. will not be deleted or changed.

2 Click Next to accept and apply the recommended restore point.

3 Click Finish.

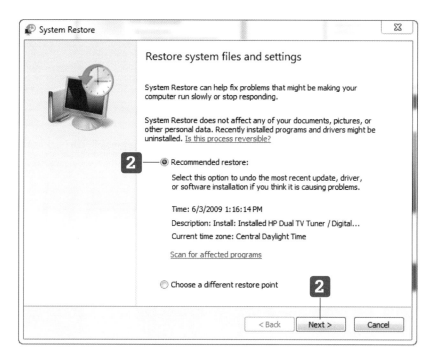

ALERT: If running System Restore on a computer, make sure it's plugged in. System Restore should never be interrupted.

HOT TIP: Many problems occur due to loose or disconnected cables. A mouse can't work unless it's plugged in or its wireless component is. A cable modem can't work unless it's connected securely to the computer and the wall. When troubleshooting, always check your connections.

WHAT DOES THIS MEAN?

Restore point: a snapshot of the Registry and system state that can be used to make an unstable computer stable again.

Registry: a part of the operating system that contains information about hardware configuration and settings, user configuration and preferences, software configuration and preferences, and other system-specific information.

1 Get to know Windows 7

Introduction

Welcome to the world of computing, and congratulations on your new Windows 7 PC; you're in for a treat and a few surprises too! No matter what your experience level, Windows 7 makes it easier than ever for you, a member of the over 50s crowd, to get started quickly and effortlessly, and to use the computer successfully no matter how much or how little you know.

You don't have to be a teenager or a 30-something to use Windows 7; in fact, you don't have to know anything at all. Its interface is intuitive. The Start button offers a place to access just about everything you'll need, from photos to music to email; the Recycle Bin holds stuff you've deleted; and the desktop offers *gadgets* you can add, like a clock, the weather and news headlines.

In this first chapter you'll learn enough to get started with Windows 7. If you've had some computing experience before, you'll probably already know much of what is explained here. If you're new to computing, there are some basics you need to know, like how to open a folder or subfolder, application or window, and how to move around inside windows. You'll learn all that here.

Important: Windows 7 manufacturers often add their own touches to a PC before they ship it. As a result, your screen may not look exactly like what you'll see in the screenshots in this book (but it'll be close).

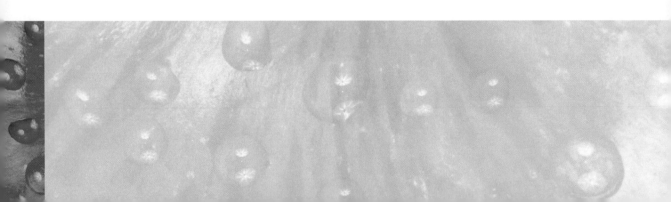

Start Windows 7

Windows 7 is the most important software installed on your computer. Although you probably have other software programs (like Microsoft Office), Windows 7 is your computer's *operating system* and this is what allows *you* to *operate* your computer's *system*. You will use Windows 7 to find things you have stored on your computer, connect to the Internet, move the mouse and see the pointer move on the screen, and print, among other things. The operating system is what allows you to communicate with your PC. Before you can use Windows 7, you have to start it.

1 If applicable, open the laptop's lid.

2 Press the Start button to turn on the computer.

3 If applicable, press the Start button on the computer monitor.

! ALERT: It takes a minute or so for the computer to start. Be patient!

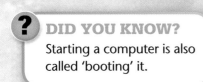

? DID YOU KNOW?
Starting a computer is also called 'booting' it.

Activate Windows 7

You have to activate Windows 7, and this is generally done over the Internet and automatically. You can find out if you have activated Windows 7 from the Activate Windows, well, window.

1 Click the Start button. It's the big round button on the bottom left of the screen.

2 Type Activation.

3 You'll see some search results, perhaps similar to what's shown here. Click Activate Windows.

4 If activation is already completed, you'll see a message stating that activation was successful. If not, you'll see the screen here. Click Activate Windows online now to continue.

! ALERT: To activate and register Windows 7 during the initial set-up, you'll have to be connected to the Internet. Alternatively, you can use the phone number provided to activate over the phone.

? DID YOU KNOW?
Activation is mandatory, and if you do not activate Windows 7 within the 30-day time frame it will lose almost all functionality – except for the activation process.

Learn what's new in Windows 7

The first time you start your computer, the Getting Started window may open. There are several sections including but not limited to Go online to find out what's new in Windows 7, Personalize Windows, Transfer files from another computer, and Back up your files. Computer manufacturers may add their own listings and links to help you learn about your computer and the applications they've installed, as well as links to their own Help files or website. From the Getting Started window you can learn what's new in Windows 7, among other things.

1 Click Start, and click Getting Started.

2 Click Go online to find out what's new in Windows 7. (If you don't have an Internet connection yet, come back to this when you do.)

3 Browse the web site as desired.

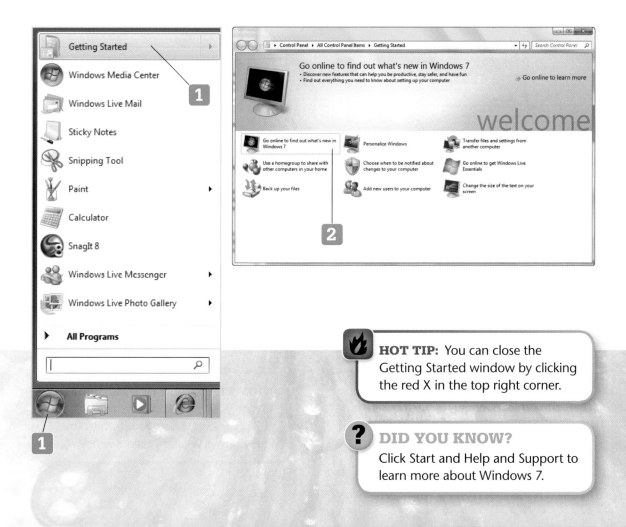

HOT TIP: You can close the Getting Started window by clicking the red X in the top right corner.

DID YOU KNOW?
Click Start and Help and Support to learn more about Windows 7.

Open your personal folder

You store the data you want to keep in your personal folder. Your data includes documents, pictures, music, contacts, videos, and more. The Start menu offers a place to access this folder easily, as well as installed programs, Windows 7 features and applications (like the Calculator, Notepad and Internet Explorer), recent items you've accessed and Games, among other things.

1 Click Start.

2 Click your user name.

3 View the items in your personal folder.

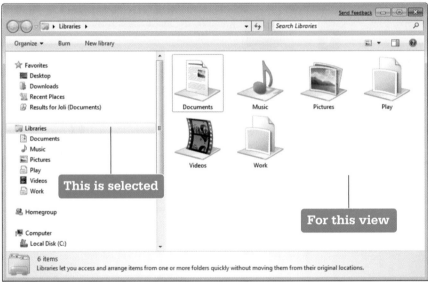

This is selected

For this view

? DID YOU KNOW?

You can click on anything you see in the Start menu to open it, and then close it using the X in the top right corner of the program window. Don't worry – you can't hurt anything!

HOT TIP: Double-click any folder inside your personal folder to open it. Click the back arrow to return to the previous view (also called a window).

Open a subfolder

Most folders that you will open will have other folders inside them. These are called subfolders. You open a subfolder in the same way as a main folder, by double-clicking. Since you'll be going 'deeper' into the folder when you do this, you'll want to click the 'Back' button to work your way back out.

1 Click Start, and click your name in the Start menu. This opens your personal folder.

2 Double-click any subfolder to open it. Here, I've clicked Favorites in the Navigation pane, and selected Contacts to view the contacts listed on my computer.

3 Click the Back button to return to your personal folder.

? DID YOU KNOW?
You can also right-click any folder and choose Open. Right-clicking opens the 'contextual' menu, a hidden menu with exceptionally useful options.

🔥 HOT TIP: Note the Search area just underneath the red X in the top right corner of the window. You can type anything there to search for it in the present window.

Close a folder or window

Each time you click an icon in the Start menu, All Programs menu or on the desktop, a window opens to display its contents. The window will stay open until you close it. To close a window, click the X in the top right corner of it.

1 Click Start.

2 Click your user name. Your personal folder opens.

3 Click the X in the top right corner to close it.

Minimise button

3

Close

HOT TIP: If you don't want to close the window but instead want to simply hide it, click the Minimise button. It's the dash to the left of the X in the top right corner.

Open an application or program

Programs (also called applications or software) offer computer users, like you, a way to perform tasks like writing letters or editing photos. You open programs that are installed on your computer from the Start menu. Once a program is open, you can access its tools to perform tasks. For instance, if you open Wordpad and type a letter to your grandchildren, you can use the interface options to change the font, font colour, or font size.

1 Click Start.

2 Click All Programs.

3 Click Desktop Gadget Gallery to open the application. Note that the Desktop Gadget Gallery lets you drag 'gadgets' to your desktop. You'll learn more about this in Chapter 2.

4 Click the X in the top right corner to close the application.

HOT TIP: You will open other programs in the same manner as that shown on this page.

DID YOU KNOW?
To close most third-party programs, you can also click File and then Exit.

Explore application windows

All windows have options. Some are menus, some icons and some are simply words you can click, but all offer ways to perform a task. For instance, when you open a window that has pictures in it, and you select a picture, you'll see the option to print or preview.

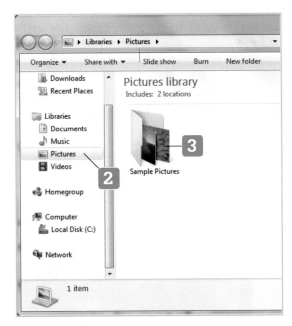

1 Click Start; click Pictures.

2 Click Pictures in the Navigation pane on the left.

3 Double-click the Sample Pictures folder to open it.

4 Single-click any picture to select it.

5 Notice the options on the toolbar: Organize, Preview, Share with, Slide show, Print, E-mail, and Burn, among others.

? DID YOU KNOW?

If you double-click a picture it will open in Windows Photo Viewer.

? DID YOU KNOW?

Burn means to copy the data to a CD.

Minimise a window

When you have several open windows, you may want to minimise (hide) the windows you aren't using. A minimised window appears on the taskbar as a small icon, and is not on the desktop. When you're ready to use the window again, you simply click it.

1 Open any window. (Click Start, and then click Pictures, Documents, Games, or any other option.)

2 Click the – sign in the top right corner; that's the Minimise button. If it's hard for you to click the Minimise button see the Hot Tip.

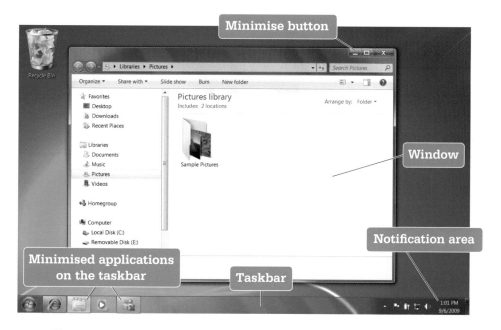

HOT TIP: Click the top of any open window and 'shake' it, by holding down the left mouse key and dragging the mouse left and right. This will minimise all open windows except the one you are 'shaking'.

WHAT DOES THIS MEAN?

Taskbar: the light blue bar that runs across the bottom of your screen. It contains the Start button and the Notification area.

Notification area: the far right portion of the taskbar that holds the clock, volume and other system icons.

Restore a window

When a window is in restore mode, you can manually resize or move it. If the icon next to the X in the top right corner of a window is a single square, the window is already in restore mode, and the only thing you can do is minimise or maximise it.

1 Open any application or folder.

2 In the top right corner of the window, locate the two square buttons.

3 Click the button to put the window in restore mode.

HOT TIP: If the window is maximised and taking up the entire screen, drag from the top of the window downwards to put it in restore mode.

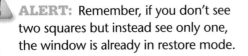

 ALERT: Remember, if you don't see two squares but instead see only one, the window is already in restore mode.

HOT TIP: When a window is maximised, you can click its title bar and drag it to put it in restore mode.

Maximise a window

A maximised window is as large as it can be, and takes up the entire screen. You can maximise a window that is on the desktop by clicking the square icon in the top right corner. If the icon is already a square, it's already maximised.

1 Open a window.

2 In the top right corner of the window, locate the square.

3 Click it to maximise the window.

 HOT TIP: You can drag any window towards the top of the screen to maximise it, and from the top down to restore it.

 HOT TIP: If a window is not maximised you can resize it by dragging from any corner of the window inwards or outwards.

 ALERT: Remember, if you see two squares instead of one, the window is already maximised.

Move a window

You can move a window no matter what its mode. You move a window by dragging it from its titlebar. The titlebar is the bar that runs across the top of the window. Moving windows allows you to position multiple windows across the screen.

1 Open any window.

2 Left-click with the mouse on the titlebar and drag. Let go of the mouse when the window is positioned correctly.

? DID YOU KNOW?

You can open a document or a picture and it will open in a window.

HOT TIP: Try dragging a window almost all the way off the screen to the left or right. It will automatically position itself to take up half of the screen.

HOT TIP: Drag and shake any window to minimise all of the other windows automatically.

Resize a window

Resizing a window allows you to change the dimensions of the window. You can resize a window by dragging from its sides, corners, or the top and bottom.

1 Open any window. (If you're unsure, click Start, and Pictures.)

2 Put the window in restore mode. You want the maximise button to show.

3 Position the mouse at one of the window corners, so that the mouse pointer becomes a two-pointed arrow.

4 Hold down the mouse button and drag the arrow to resize the window.

5 Repeat as desired, dragging from the sides, top, bottom or corners.

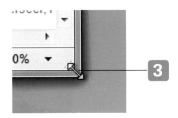

ALERT: You can only manually resize windows if they are in restore mode, meaning the maximise button is showing in the top right corner of the window.

Shut down Windows safely

When you're ready to turn off your computer, you need to do so using the method detailed here. Simply pressing the power button can damage the computer and/or the operating system.

1 Click Start.

2 Click Shut down.

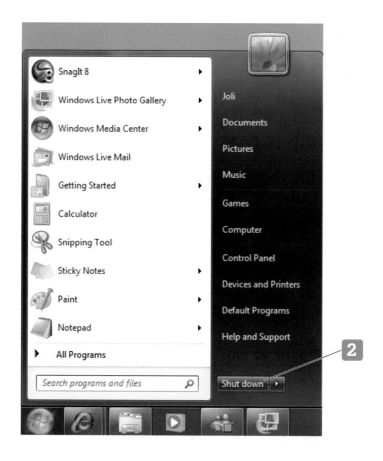

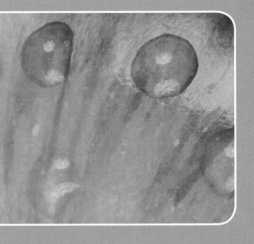

2 Personalise Windows 7

Introduction

In order to make your new Windows 7 computer your own, you'll need to personalise it with a new background, screen saver and desktop icons. Personalising isn't just aesthetic though; making custom changes can make the computer easier to use. For instance, if you have trouble seeing the desktop icons because they are too small, you can make them larger. If you want to rotate your desktop background picture every 30 minutes so you can see your grandchildren's pictures, you can do that too. In addition, you can add gadgets to the desktop so you can get real-time information on the weather or stock prices, and you can use keyboard shortcuts to move between windows, minimising how often you have to click the tiny Minimise and Maximise buttons in the corner of open windows to manage them.

Change the desktop background

One of the first things you might want to do when you get a new PC or upgrade an older one is to personalise the picture on the desktop. That picture is called the background. You can make the background a solid colour if you have trouble seeing the desktop icons or you can select a background that simply suits your taste.

1 Right-click an empty area of the desktop.

2 Click Personalize.

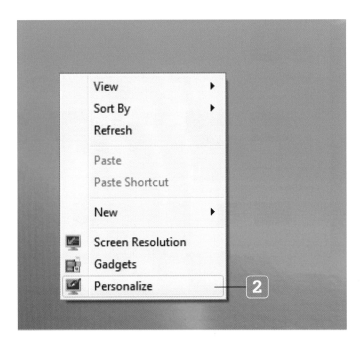

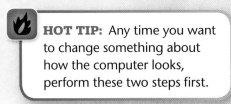 **HOT TIP:** Any time you want to change something about how the computer looks, perform these two steps first.

3 Click Desktop Background.

4 Windows Desktop Backgrounds is selected by default, but there are others, shown here. Choose a location.

5 Select any picture, and note that the desktop changes automatically.

6 Click Save changes.

HOT TIP: Click the red X in the top right corner of the Personalization window to close it.

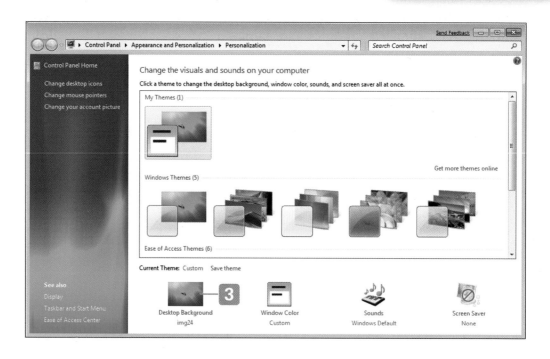

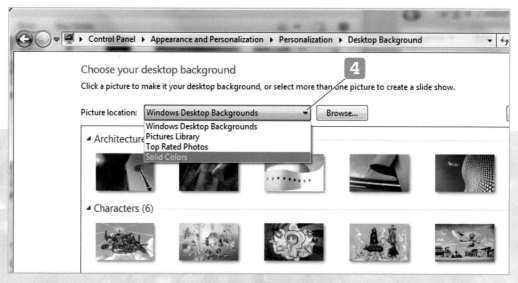

Configure a rotating background with your favourite pictures

You can configure the desktop background to change automatically. The time intervals you can select range from every 10 seconds to once a day. You can use the pictures that come with Windows 7 or you can choose a folder of your own. You might want to create a folder that contains pictures of your family, and use that as your background.

1 Right-click an empty area of the desktop and click Personalize.

2 Click Desktop Background.

3 Select the picture to use or click Select all to select every one. Next, choose how often to change the picture.

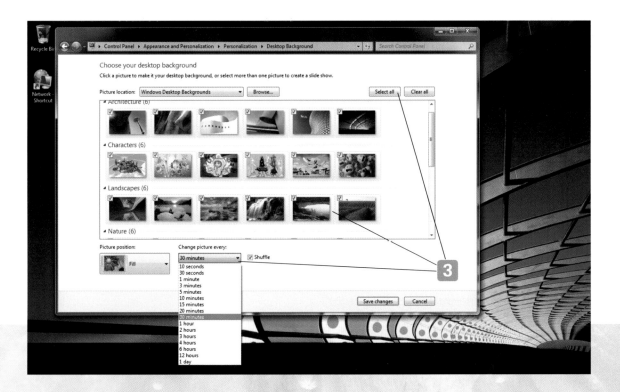

4 Click Save changes.

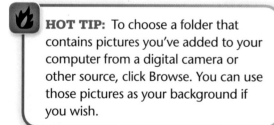

HOT TIP: To choose a folder that contains pictures you've added to your computer from a digital camera or other source, click Browse. You can use those pictures as your background if you wish.

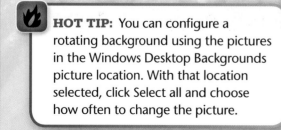

HOT TIP: You can configure a rotating background using the pictures in the Windows Desktop Backgrounds picture location. With that location selected, click Select all and choose how often to change the picture.

Change the screen saver

A screen saver is a picture or animation that covers your screen and appears after your computer has been idle for a specific amount of time that you set. Screen savers are used for either visual enhancement or as a security feature. For security, you can configure your screen saver to require a password on waking up, which happens when you move the mouse or hit a key on the keyboard. Requiring a password means that once the screen saver is running, no one, not even your teenagers or grandchildren, can log onto your computer by typing in your password when prompted.

1 Right-click an empty area of the desktop.

2 Click Personalize.

3 Click Screen Savers.

? DID YOU KNOW?

Select Photos and your screen saver will be a slide show of photos stored in your Pictures folder.

4 Click the arrow to see the available screen saver and select one.

5 Use the arrows to change how long to wait before the screen saver is enabled.

6 If desired, click On resume, display logon screen to require a password to log back into the computer.

7 Click OK.

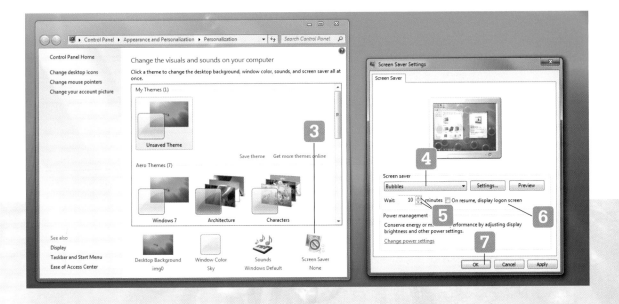

Add desktop icons

When Windows 7 started the first time, it may have had only one item on the desktop, the Recycle Bin. Alternatively, it may have had 20 or more. What appears on your desktop the first time Windows boots up depends on a number of factors, including who manufactured and/or installed the PC.

1 Right-click an empty area of the desktop.

2 Click Personalize.

3 Click Change desktop icons.

4 Select the desktop icons you want to appear on your desktop.

5 Click OK.

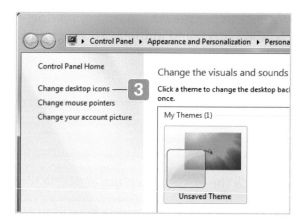

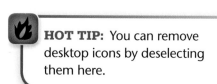

HOT TIP: You can remove desktop icons by deselecting them here.

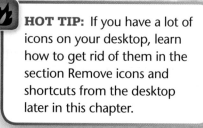

HOT TIP: If you have a lot of icons on your desktop, learn how to get rid of them in the section Remove icons and shortcuts from the desktop later in this chapter.

Change the size of desktop icons

If you have trouble seeing the icons on the desktop, you can change their size. When you make the change detailed here, you'll also change the size of the text and other items on the screen, including the Start menu.

1 Click Start, and in the Start Search box, type display.

2 Click Display.

3 Select a display option.

4 Click Apply.

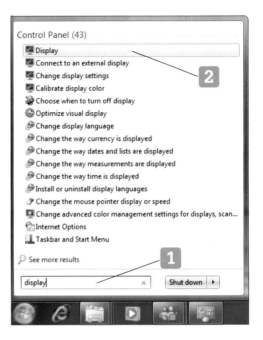

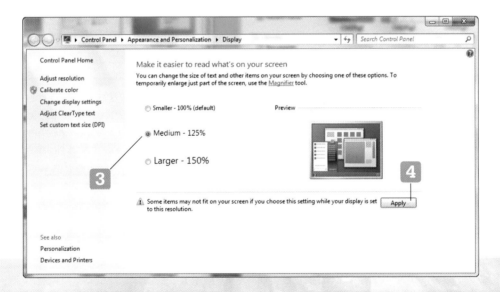

HOT TIP: You'll have to restart the PC or log off and log back on for the changes to take effect.

ALERT: If you choose a larger size, the items you're used to seeing may not all fit on your screen any more. If this happens, consider changing the size back.

Create a desktop shortcut for a program or application

If you are tired of clicking the Start button to locate a program you use often, you can create a shortcut for it on your desktop. Shortcuts you place on the desktop let you access folders, files, programs and other items by double-clicking an icon. Shortcuts always appear with an arrow beside them (or on them, actually). To create a shortcut for a program installed on your computer, you'll have to find it in the All Programs menu first, as detailed here.

1 Click Start, and then click All Programs.

2 Locate the program you'd like to create a shortcut for and right-click it.

3 Click Send To.

4 Click Desktop (create shortcut).

HOT TIP: You can create a shortcut for a file, folder, picture, song or other item by locating it and right-clicking, as detailed in this section.

ALERT: You can delete a shortcut by dragging it to the Recycle Bin. Be careful though; only delete shortcuts – don't delete any actual folders!

Remove icons and shortcuts from the desktop

When you're ready to remove items from the desktop, you'll use the right-click method again. The options you'll have when you right-click an item on the desktop will differ depending on what type of icon you select. You can delete shortcuts and Windows 7 icons like Computer and Network safely, but be careful that you don't delete any actual data you want to keep. Make sure you always read the warning before deleting.

Note: If your brand new PC has lots of icons on the desktop, that means the computer manufacturer installed lots of programs. You may want to use those programs (or you may want to uninstall them from Control Panel). So, before you start deleting shortcuts, make sure you understand what each icon represents and what is available to you.

1 Right-click the icon to remove.

2 Click Delete.

3 Read the warning and click Yes to complete the deletion.

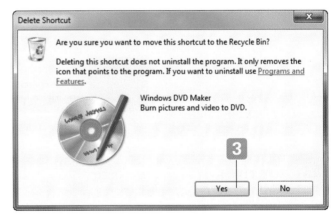

ALERT: If you are deleting a shortcut, you might see a warning that you are moving a file to the Recycle Bin, when in reality you are not. Remember, if it has an arrow by it, it's a shortcut and can be deleted.

HOT TIP: Even if you accidentally delete something you want to keep, you can find and restore it, from the Recycle Bin.

Restore data using the Recycle Bin

If you delete something that you decide you later want to keep or need, you can 'restore' it from the Recycle Bin.

1 Double-click the Recycle Bin.

2 Right-click the file, shortcut, folder or data to recover.

3 Click Restore.

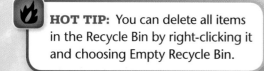
HOT TIP: You can only restore an item from the Recycle Bin if it's still in there. If you have emptied the Recycle Bin since deleting the item, it's gone for ever.

HOT TIP: You can delete all items in the Recycle Bin by right-clicking it and choosing Empty Recycle Bin.

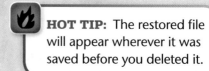
HOT TIP: The restored file will appear wherever it was saved before you deleted it.

Change the view in a window

Another way to make the computer easier to access is to change how you view items in a window. You can configure each folder independently so that the data appears in a list, as small icons or as large icons, to name a few. If you choose to view the items as icons, you'll be able to see a thumbnail of the item without actually opening it.

1 Click Start; click Pictures.

2 Click Pictures in the Navigation panel and double-click the Sample Pictures folder.

3 Locate the Views button.

? DID YOU KNOW?

You can also click a choice on the slider to make a view selection.

4 Click the arrow next to Views and make a selection using the slider.

5 Locate the Preview button. Click it to show the Preview pane.

🔥 **HOT TIP:** Show items in the Pictures folder as large or extra large icons, and you'll be able to tell what each picture looks like without actually opening it in a program.

🔥 **HOT TIP:** To see the old-fashioned menus, click the Alt key on the keyboard. From there, you can select View, and choose from a familiar drop-down list.

Use Flip

Windows Flip offers a quick way to choose a specific window when multiple windows are open. With Flip, you can scroll through open windows until you land on the one you want to use, and then select it.

1 With multiple windows open, on the keyboard, hold down the Alt key with one finger (or thumb).

2 While holding down the Alt key, press the Tab key.

3 Press the Tab key again (making sure that the Alt key is still depressed).

4 When the item you want to bring to the front is selected let go of the Tab key, and then let go of the Alt key.

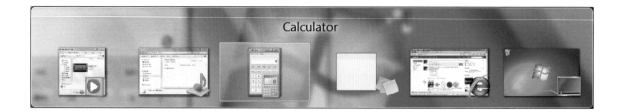

Calculator

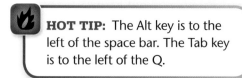

HOT TIP: The Alt key is to the left of the space bar. The Tab key is to the left of the Q.

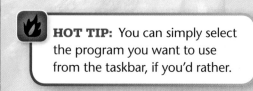

HOT TIP: You can simply select the program you want to use from the taskbar, if you'd rather.

Use Flip 3D

Windows Flip 3D offers a quick way to choose a specific window when multiple windows are open. With Flip, you can scroll through open windows until you land on the one you want to use, and then select it.

1 With multiple windows open, on the keyboard, hold down the Windows key (which may have Start written on it) with one finger (or thumb).

2 Click the Tab key once, while keeping the Windows key depressed.

3 Press the Tab key again (making sure that the Windows key is still depressed) to scroll through the open windows.

4 When the item you want to bring to the front is selected let go of the Tab key, and then let go of the Windows key.

 HOT TIP: The Windows key is the key to the left of the space bar and has the Windows logo printed on it.

 ALERT: If Flip 3D doesn't work, or if you get only Flip and not Flip 3D, you need to enable a Windows theme in the Personalization options.

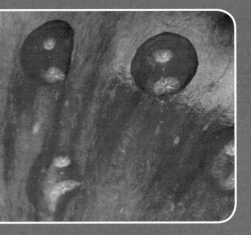

3 Work with programs

Introduction

You're probably anxious to start doing things, like writing and printing letters. Windows 7 comes with two programs to help you do that: Notepad and WordPad. It can also help you balance your bank book: there's an easy-to-use calculator too. There's a tool for copying and emailing any part of your screen, and a program called Sound Recorder for recording voice clips as well. These applications, like so many others, can help you perform and complete everyday tasks, and they all come preinstalled in Windows 7. There are games, like Solitaire, among others. Let's get started!

Search for a program from the Start menu

The Start button and the resulting Start menu is your ticket to anything stored anywhere on the computer. From the Start menu you can search for programs and data using the Start Search window, open personal folders or browse the All Programs list to see the programs and accessories installed on your PC.

1 Click Start.

2 In the Start Search window, type anything that represents what you're looking for.

3 Select the item you're looking for from the results.

HOT TIP: The fastest way to find something on your PC, whether it's a document, picture or program, is to type what you're looking for in the Start Search window.

DID YOU KNOW?
You can search for a word inside a document and the results will appear. For instance, Bocce is a word listed in the document My favorite outdoor games and thus appears in the results.

Write a letter with Notepad

If you need to create and print a simple document like a grocery or to-do list, or need to put together a weekly newsletter that you send via email, there's no reason to purchase a large office suite like Microsoft Office (and learn how to use it) when Notepad will do just fine. Although you can't create and insert tables, add endnotes, add text boxes or perform similar tasks with Notepad, you may never need to anyway.

1 Click Start.

2 In the Start Search window, type Notepad.

3 Click Notepad under Programs. (Note that you may see other results, as shown here.)

4 Click once inside Notepad, and start typing.

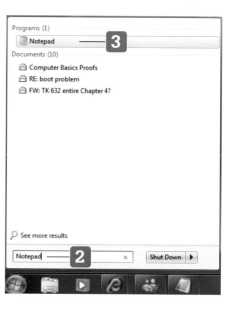

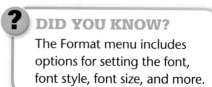

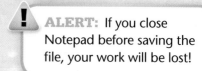

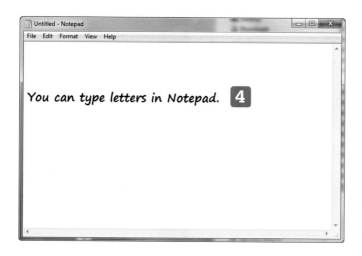

? **DID YOU KNOW?**
The Format menu includes options for setting the font, font style, font size, and more.

! **ALERT:** Notepad has five menus: File, Edit, Format, View and Help. After you become familiar with these menus, what you learn will carry over to almost any other program you'll use.

! **ALERT:** If you close Notepad before saving the file, your work will be lost!

Save a letter with Notepad

If you want to save a letter you've written in Notepad so you can work with it later, you have to click File and then click Save. This will allow you to name the file and save it to your hard drive. The next time you want to view the file, you can click File and then click Open if Notepad is already open, or you can search for the name of the file from the Start Search window, click it and Notepad will open automatically.

1 Click File.

2 Click Save.

3 Type a name for the file. Notice that the default folder for saving a Notepad document is Documents library.

4 Click Save.

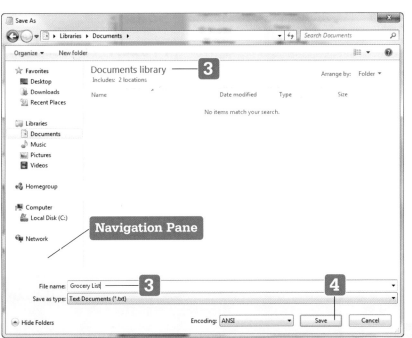

Navigation Pane

🔥 HOT TIP: You can access the Documents folder from the Start menu.

🔥 HOT TIP: You can reopen a saved file and make changes to it, and then resave it. Your changes will be saved as well.

🔥 HOT TIP: You can change the folder by selecting another one from the left pane, called the Navigation pane. You could choose Desktop if you want the file to be saved directly to the desktop, for instance.

Print a letter with Notepad

Sometimes you'll need to print a letter so you can mail it, or print a grocery list for shopping. You can access the Print command from the File menu.

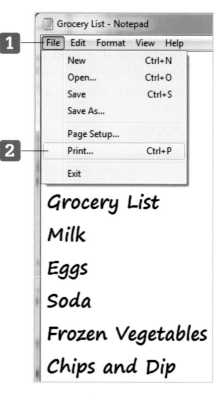

1 Click File.

2 Click Print.

3 Select a printer (if more than one exists).

4 Click Print.

HOT TIP: You can locate the saved file in the Documents folder if you accepted the default Save option, or you can search for the file by typing its name or any word in it from the Start Search window.

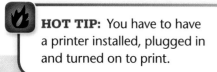

HOT TIP: You have to have a printer installed, plugged in and turned on to print.

WHAT DOES THIS MEAN?

Printer Preferences: lets you select the page orientation, print order and the type of paper you'll be printing on, among other features.

Page Range: lets you select what pages to print.

Use the calculator

You've probably used a calculator before, and using the Windows 7 calculator is not much different from a hand held one, except that you input numbers with a mouse click, keyboard, or a number pad. There are four calculators available, and Standard is the default.

1 Click Start, and in the Start Search window, type Calculator.

2 In the Programs results, click Calculator.

3 Input numbers using the keypad or by clicking the on-screen calculator with the mouse.

4 Input operations using the keypad or by clicking the on-screen calculator with the mouse.

5 Close Calculator by clicking the X in the top right corner of it.

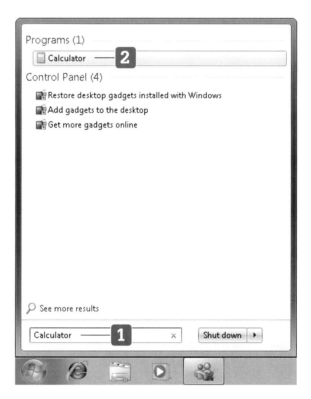

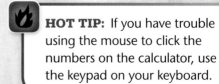

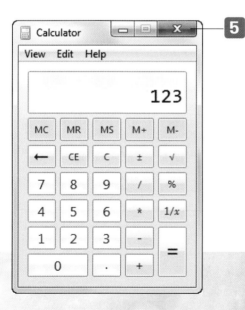

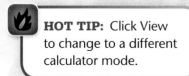
HOT TIP: Click View to change to a different calculator mode.

HOT TIP: If you have trouble using the mouse to click the numbers on the calculator, use the keypad on your keyboard.

Take a screenshot

Sometimes you'll see something on your screen you want to capture to keep or share. It may be part of a webpage (like a picture of a great pair of shoes or a new car), or an error message you want to share with your grandchild (who can probably resolve it). The Snipping Tool lets you capture the shot. To use the Snipping Tool, you drag your mouse cursor around any area on the screen to copy and capture it. Once captured, you can save it, edit it and/or send it to an email recipient.

1 Click Start.

2 In the Start Search dialogue box, type Snip.

3 Under Programs, select Snipping Tool.

4 Drag your mouse across any part of the screen. When you let go of the mouse, the snip will appear in the Snipping Tool window.

5 Click Tools, and click Pen, to access the pen options. You can use the pen to draw on the snip.

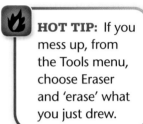

HOT TIP: If you mess up, from the Tools menu, choose Eraser and 'erase' what you just drew.

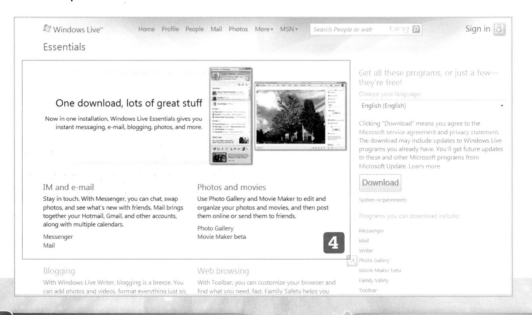

HOT TIP: Editing tools will become available after creating a snip. You can write on a clip with a red, blue, black or customised pen or a highlighter, and if you mess up, you can use the eraser.

ALERT: If you want to keep the snip you'll have to save it. Click File, and click Save As to name the file and save it to your hard drive.

Email a screenshot

You can use the Snipping Tool to take a picture of your screen as detailed in the previous section. You can even write on it with a 'pen'. You can also email that screenshot if you'd like to share it with someone.

1 Take a screenshot with the Snipping Tool.

2 Click File, and click Send To.

3 Click E-mail Recipient.

4 Insert the recipients' names, change the subject if desired, type a message if desired, and click Send.

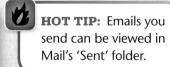

ALERT: If you select E-mail Recipient, this will insert the snip inside an email. Note that you can also send the snip as an attachment.

SEE ALSO: For more information on sending an email, refer to Chapter 9.

HOT TIP: Emails you send can be viewed in Mail's 'Sent' folder.

Play Solitaire

Windows 7 comes with lots of games. You access the available games from the Games folder on the Start menu. Each game offers instructions on how to play it and, for the most part, moving a player, tile or card, dealing a card, or otherwise moving around the screen is performed using the mouse. One of the most popular games around is Solitaire.

1 Click Start.

2 Click Games.

3 Double-click Solitaire to begin the game.

4 Double-click any card to move it or drag the card to the desired location.

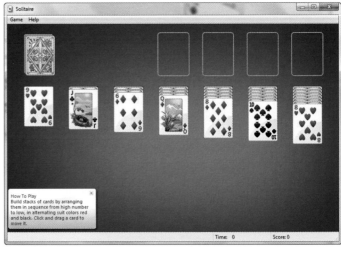

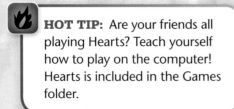

HOT TIP: Are your friends all playing Hearts? Teach yourself how to play on the computer! Hearts is included in the Games folder.

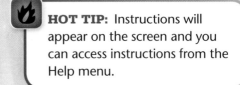

HOT TIP: Instructions will appear on the screen and you can access instructions from the Help menu.

Record a sound clip

Sometimes the spoken word is best. With the Sound Recorder, you can record a quick note to yourself, your partner or your children, instead of writing a letter or sending an email. Sound Recorder is a simple tool with only three options, Start Recording, Stop Recording and Resume Recording. To record, click Start Recording; to stop, click Stop Recording; to continue, click Resume Recording. You save your recording as a Windows Media Audio file, which will play by default in Windows Media Player.

1 Click Start.

2 In the Start Search dialogue box, type Sound Recorder.

3 Under Programs, click Sound Recorder.

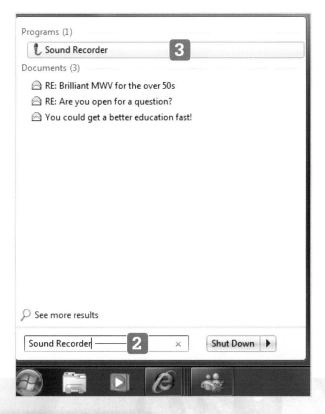

HOT TIP: You can use your saved recording in Movie Maker and other Windows-related programs, email the clip, and you can save and play the clip on almost any media player.

4 Click Start Recording and speak into your microphone.

5 Click Stop Recording to complete the recording.

6 In the Save As dialogue box, type a name for your recording and click Save.

7 Click the X in the Sound Recorder to close it.

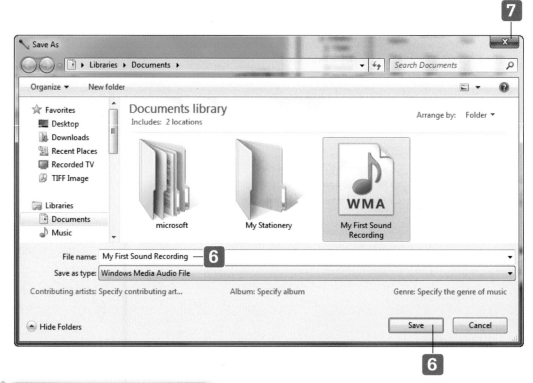

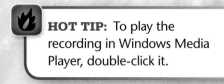

ALERT: You can't record anything without a microphone.

HOT TIP: To play the recording in Windows Media Player, double-click it.

4 Install hardware and software

Introduction

After a bit of time with your new PC, you'll probably decide to purchase additional 'hardware' like a printer or scanner, and you may already have hardware you want to install, like a digital camera, mobile phone, microphone or headphones. When you connect a piece of hardware like this, the first thing Windows 7 will try to do is install a *driver* for it. A driver is a special kind of software that allows the device to communicate with Windows 7 and vice versa. Drivers are different from the software you're familiar with though, and it's important to know the difference.

In this chapter, you'll learn how to physically install printers, cameras, and other hardware, and how to allow them to communicate with Windows 7 using drivers. You'll also learn when to install the additional software that comes with your new hardware and when not to!

Note: You should always read the directions that come with a new device, like a printer or mobile phone. However, in almost all cases, you will connect the device, turn it on and wait for the device to be automatically installed. In rare cases, you may need to follow prompts to complete the installation.

Install a printer or scanner

Printer installation is almost always a straightforward affair. You connect the device to the PC, plug it in, turn it on, and wait while the driver installs automatically. Windows 7 has a vast library of drivers and if it can't find what it needs, it'll check for the driver online.

1 Connect the printer to a wall outlet.

2 Connect the printer to the PC using either a USB cable or a parallel port cable.

3 Insert the CD for the device, if you have it. However, if a pop-up message appears regarding the CD, click the X to close the window.

4 Turn on the device.

5 Wait while the driver is installed and you will see the message shown here.

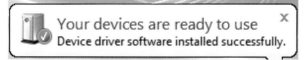

 DID YOU KNOW?
The reason you should let Windows 7 install a device on its own is because when you install a CD that comes with a device, you'll probably also install applications you'll never use and don't need.

 HOT TIP: If, after using the printer a few times, you need to access advanced printer preferences like printing in reverse or applying light or heavy ink, insert the printer CD again and install only the printer software (and nothing else).

ALERT: You only need intervene in a hardware installation when Windows 7 can't install the device on its own. Almost always, this simply involves inserting the CD that came with the device.

Install a digital camera or webcam

As you would when installing a printer or scanner, to install a camera you insert the CD that came with the camera, plug in the new hardware and turn it on, and wait for Windows 7 to install your hardware.

1 Read the directions that came with the camera. If there are specific instructions for installing the driver, follow them. If not, continue here.

2 Connect the camera to a wall outlet or insert fresh batteries, and connect the camera to the PC using either a USB cable or a FireWire cable.

3 Insert the CD for the device, if you have it; if a pop-up message appears, click the X to close the window.

4 Turn on the camera. Place it in Playback mode if that exists. Often, simply turning on the camera is enough.

5 Wait while the driver is installed.

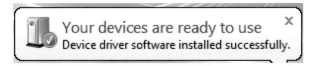

Your devices are ready to use   x
Device driver software installed successfully.

6 You'll see the camera in the Computer window (click Start, click Computer).

! ALERT: It's usually best to connect the new camera, turn it on and let Windows 7 install it. You only need intervene when Windows 7 can't install the hardware on its own.

? DID YOU KNOW?
When you install everything on the CD that comes with your camera, you're probably installing applications you'll never use and don't need.

WHAT DOES THIS MEAN?

Driver: software that allows the PC and the new hardware to communicate with each other.

USB: a technology used to connect hardware to a PC. A USB cable is often used to connect a digital camera to a PC.

FireWire: a technology used to connect hardware to a PC. A FireWire cable is a cable often used to connect a digital video camera to a PC.

 DID YOU KNOW?
Even if you aren't installing the CD, leave the CD in the drive. If Windows 7 wants information on the CD, it will acquire it from there.

ALERT: If the camera does not install properly, refer to the camera's user manual.

Install other hardware

For hardware other than printers or cameras, perform the same steps. Insert a driver CD if one came with the hardware, plug in the new hardware and turn it on, and wait for Windows 7 to install the required driver. If Windows 7 can't find the driver it needs on the CD or in its own driver database on the hard drive, it will connect to the Internet and look for the driver in Microsoft's online driver database. Almost all of the time, Windows 7 will be successful using one of these methods. For the most part, speakers, headphones, printers, scanners and digital cameras all install this way.

1 Connect the hardware to a PC and/or a wall outlet.

2 Insert the CD for the device, if you have it.

3 If a pop-up message appears regarding the CD, click the X to close the window.

4 Turn on the device.

5 Wait while the driver is installed.

6 If you receive a message that the driver was not successfully installed, click the message to see why and how to resolve the issue.

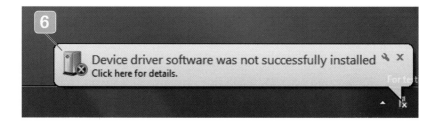

6

Device driver software was not successfully installed
Click here for details.

ALERT: When the instructions for a hardware device tell you to insert the CD before connecting the hardware, it's often just a ruse to get you to install unnecessary software, so be aware of what you're installing.

ALERT: On occasion, hardware manufacturers will require you to install software first, and then plug in the device, and then turn on the hardware, so read the instructions that came with your hardware to know in what order to do what, just as a precaution.

Locate a driver

As noted, almost all of the time, hardware installs automatically and with no input from you (other than plugging it in and turning it on). However, in rare cases, the hardware does not install properly or is simply not available. If this happens, you'll be informed that the hardware did not install and may not work properly. If you cannot replace the device with something Windows 7 recognises, you'll have to locate and install the driver yourself.

1 Write down the name and model number of the device.

2 Open Internet Explorer and locate the manufacturer's website.

3 Locate a link for Support, Support and Drivers, Customer Support, or something similar. Click it.

4 Locate your device driver by make, model, or other characteristics.

 HOT TIP: The make and model of a device are probably located on the bottom of the device.

 HOT TIP: To find the manufacturer's website, try putting a www. before the company name and a .com after. (www.epson.com, www.hewlett-packard.com and www.apple.com are examples.)

ALERT: Locating a driver is the first step. You must now download the driver and later install it.

Download and install a driver

If you've located the driver you need, you can now download and install it. Downloading is the process of saving the driver to your computer's hard drive. Once downloaded, you can install the driver.

1 Locate the driver as detailed in the previous section.

2 Click Download Driver, Obtain Software, or something similar.

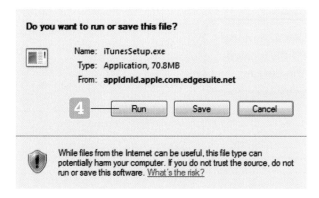

Driver

Description	Current version	Size (MB)	Estimated download time	Previous version	
HP LaserJet and Color LaserJet products - products supported and drivers included in Microsoft Windows Vista	N/A 6 Dec 2006	-	-	-	» Obtain software

3 Click Save, if prompted.

4 Click Run, Install, or Open Window to begin the installation.

5 Follow the directions in the set-up process to complete the installation.

Do you want to run or save this file?

Name: iTunesSetup.exe
Type: Application, 70.8MB
From: appldnld.apple.com.edgesuite.net

4 — Run   Save   Cancel

While files from the Internet can be useful, this file type can potentially harm your computer. If you do not trust the source, do not run or save this software. What's the risk?

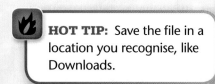

HOT TIP: Save the file in a location you recognise, like Downloads.

ALERT: If installation does not begin automatically, browse to the location of the file and double-click it to begin the installation manually.

Using ReadyBoost

ReadyBoost is a technology that lets you add more RAM (random access memory) to a PC easily, without opening the computer tower or the laptop case. Adding RAM often improves performance dramatically. ReadyBoost lets you use a USB flash drive or a secure digital memory card (like the one in your digital camera) as RAM, if it meets certain requirements.

1 Insert a USB flash drive, thumb drive, portable music player or memory card into an available slot on the outside of your PC.

2 Wait while Windows 7 checks to see if the device can perform as memory.

3 If prompted to use the flash drive or memory card to improve system performance, click Speed up my system.

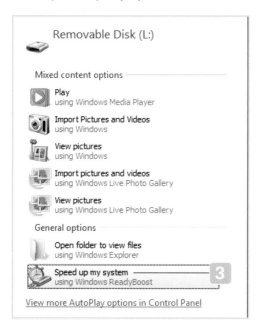

WHAT DOES THIS MEAN?

RAM: random access memory. RAM is where information is stored temporarily so the operating system has quick access to it. The more RAM you have, the better your PC should perform.

USB or thumb drive: a small device that plugs into a USB port on your PC, often for the purpose of backing up or storing files on external media.

Portable music player: often a small USB drive. This device also has a headphone jack and controls for listening to music stored on it.

Media card: a removable card used in digital cameras to store data and transfer it to the PC.

Install software

As with installing hardware, software installation goes smoothly almost every time. Just make sure you get your software from a reliable source, like Amazon, Microsoft's website, Apple's website (think iTunes, not software for Macs only) or a retail store. Downloading software from the Internet is risky, and you never know if it will run properly or contain adware or spyware. It's best simply to stay away, unless the company is well known like Adobe, and you're willing to burn your own software backup disks.

1 Insert the CD or DVD in the appropriate drive. If prompted, click Run or Install. Proceed to step 5.

2 If you are not prompted then click Start, and click Computer.

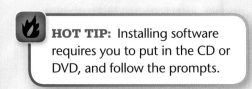

HOT TIP: Installing software requires you to put in the CD or DVD, and follow the prompts.

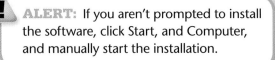

ALERT: If you aren't prompted to install the software, click Start, and Computer, and manually start the installation.

3 Right-click the CD or DVD drive.

4 Click Install or run program.

5 Work through the installation wizard.

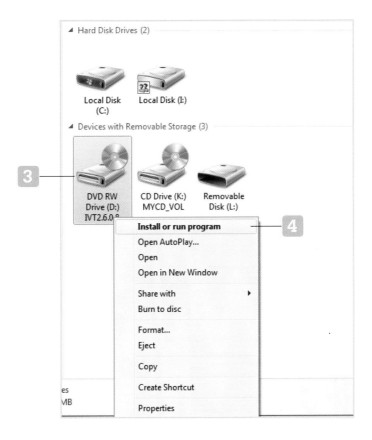

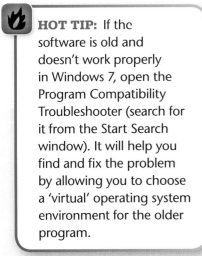

HOT TIP: If the software is old and doesn't work properly in Windows 7, open the Program Compatibility Troubleshooter (search for it from the Start Search window). It will help you find and fix the problem by allowing you to choose a 'virtual' operating system environment for the older program.

Using the Action Center

The Action Center helps you find and fix problems with hardware and software. If you were unable to resolve a particular problem by downloading and installing your own driver, check the Action Center periodically. It may have found a solution for you.

1 Click Start, and in the Start Search window type Action Center.

2 Open the Action Center.

3 Review the recent messages and resolve problems as detailed. Here you can see there is no virus protection but a way to find a program online is offered.

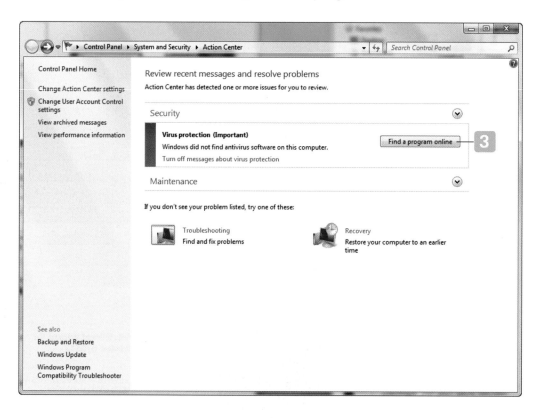

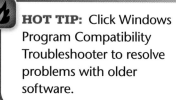

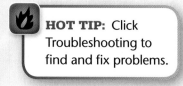
HOT TIP: Click Troubleshooting to find and fix problems.

HOT TIP: Click Recovery to restore your computer to a time when it was problem-free.

HOT TIP: Click Windows Program Compatibility Troubleshooter to resolve problems with older software.

5 Windows Live Photo Gallery

Introduction

Windows 7 comes with Windows Photo Viewer, an application that allows you to view, print, email and burn photos to a CD or DVD. Windows 7 also comes with Paint, an application that allows you to resize, rotate, outline and view photos, among other things. However, you still need to obtain a program for *editing* digital photos – removing red-eye, adjusting the colour, exposure and detail, adding effects, creating panoramic views, and performing other editing tasks.

Although you could purchase a third-party program, Windows Live Photo Gallery may be all you need to manage, manipulate, edit, view, and share your digital photos. Before you install additional software, including software on the CD that shipped with your digital camera, printer, or scanner, try this program. It's free, and only requires you to download and install it.

Download and install Windows Live Photo Gallery

You have to download and install Windows Live Photo Gallery. It's on the Internet. If you've never downloaded and/or installed a program before, you may be a little nervous about doing so. Don't worry, it's really easy, safe and secure, and Microsoft has set it up so that the process requires very little input from you. There are only a few steps: go to the website, click the Download link, and wait for the download and installation process to complete.

1 Open Internet Explorer and go to http://www.windowslive.com/Desktop/PhotoGallery.

2 Look for the Download now button and click it. You'll be prompted to click Download now once more on the next screen.

3 Click Run, and when prompted, click Yes.

4 When prompted, select the items to download. If the programs have already been installed by the computer manufacturer, you'll be informed what programs were installed and what is still available.

5 When prompted to select your settings, make the desired choices. You can't go wrong here; there are no bad options.

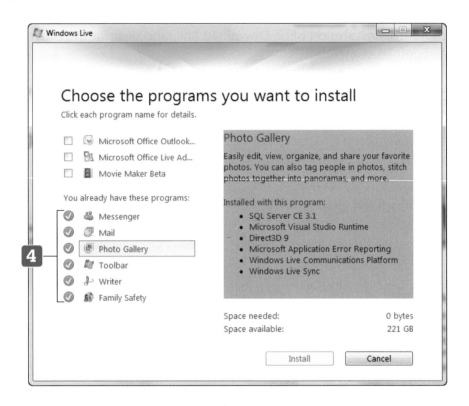

HOT TIP: During this installation process, go ahead and download Mail, Messenger and Toolbar; you'll find all three useful.

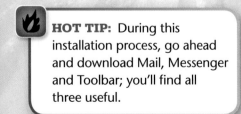
DID YOU KNOW?
It's OK to select all of these programs if you think you'll use them; they are all free. However, Family Safety can get a tad annoying, so only install that if you have children who will use your computer.

Get a Windows Live account

When you use 'Live' services, like Windows Live Photo Gallery, you log into them using a free, Windows Live account. You need a Windows Live account which provides an email address and password you use to log on to your Live programs on the Internet.

1 If you do not already have a Windows Live account, click Sign up after the installation of Live Mail completes. (You can also go to http://signup.live.com.)

2 Fill out the required information and click I accept when finished.

? DID YOU KNOW?
You can use your Windows Live email account as a regular email address, or simply use it to log into Live services on the Internet.

🔥 HOT TIP: Fill out the information with true information. This is an ID, after all.

View pictures

You can use various applications to view pictures with Windows 7, but Windows Live Photo Gallery is the best. With it, you have easy access to slide shows, editing tools and picture groupings. You can sort and filter, and organise as desired. You can even create folders for each of your grandchildren.

1 Open Windows Live Photo Gallery. If prompted, log in using your Windows Live ID.

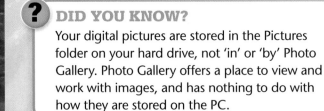

DID YOU KNOW?

Your digital pictures are stored in the Pictures folder on your hard drive, not 'in' or 'by' Photo Gallery. Photo Gallery offers a place to view and work with images, and has nothing to do with how they are stored on the PC.

2 If prompted, click Yes to associate picture file types with Windows Live Photo Gallery.

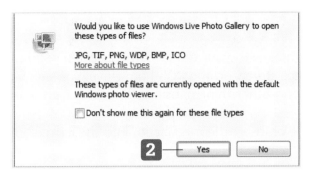

3 Notice the sample pictures. Double-click any picture to open it in a larger window.

4 Click Back to Gallery to return to the previous page.

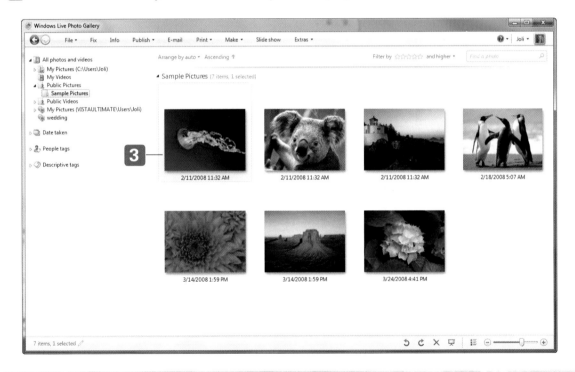

Import pictures from a digital camera or media card

After you've taken pictures with your digital camera, you'll need to move or copy those pictures to the PC. Once stored on the PC's hard drive, you can view, edit, email or print the pictures (among other things), using Windows Live Photo Gallery.

1 Connect the device or insert the media card into the card reader. If applicable, turn on the camera.

2 When prompted, choose Import pictures and videos using Windows Live Photo Gallery.

SEE ALSO: Install a digital camera or webcam in Chapter 4.

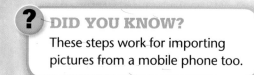

? DID YOU KNOW?

These steps work for importing pictures from a mobile phone too.

3 Click Import all new items now.

4 Type a descriptive name for the group of pictures you're importing and click Import.

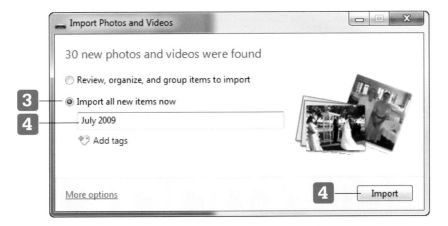

5 View your new photos.

🔥 **HOT TIP:** If desired, tick Erase after importing. This will cause Windows 7 to erase the images from the device after the import is complete.

⚠ **ALERT:** If your device isn't recognised when you plug it in and turn it on, in Windows Live Photo Gallery click File, and click Import from Camera or Scanner.

Play a slide show of pictures

1 Open Windows Live Photo Gallery.

2 Select any folder that contains pictures.

3 Click the Play Slide Show button. Wait at least three seconds.

4 To end the show, press the Esc key on the keyboard.

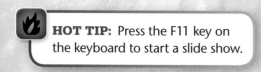

Auto adjust picture quality

With pictures on your PC and available in Windows Live Photo Gallery, you can now perform some editing. Photo Gallery offers the ability to correct brightness and contrast, colour temperature, tint and saturation, among other things.

1 Open Photo Gallery.

2 Double-click a picture to edit.

3 Click Fix.

4 Click Auto adjust to fix problems with the photo.

5 If desired, move the sliders to adjust the settings.

 HOT TIP: When you select a 'fix' option, options will appear on the right side of the screen. You can apply the options as desired.

! ALERT: After applying any option, to see more options, click the down and up arrows that will appear in the right pane.

Crop a picture

To crop means to remove parts of a picture you don't want and allows you to reposition the picture and remove extraneous parts. You can also rotate the frame.

1 Open Photo Gallery.

2 Select a picture to crop.

3 Click Fix.

4 Click Crop photo.

5 Drag the corners of the box to resize it, and drag the entire box to move it around in the picture.

6 Click Apply.

 HOT TIP: Click the arrow next to Custom to apply a preconfigured size.

 HOT TIP: Click Rotate frame to change the position of the crop box.

Add information to a picture

You can add information about a picture by adding 'tags'. Tags you create are words that describe the picture. Once tags are added, you can filter, sort and organise your pictures using these tags.

1 Open Windows Live Photo Gallery.

2 Right-click any picture and click Details.

3 Click Tags.

4 Type a tag name or several tag names separated by commas.

5 Click OK.

? DID YOU KNOW?
Some tags are applied automatically when you import pictures from a digital camera, including the date they were uploaded, along with any name you applied to the imported group.

HOT TIP: Pictures can have multiple tags. You might tag a photo as Holiday, but also apply tags that name the people in the picture, the city or the country.

HOT TIP: You'll see the new tags under Descriptive tags in the Windows Live Photo Gallery interface on the bottom left.

Email a picture

You can email photos you want to share from inside Photo Gallery. You can also choose the size to email them, and I suggest either small or medium (for best results).

1 Open Windows Live Photo Gallery.

2 Select pictures to email.

3 Click E-mail.

4 Compose the email and send it.

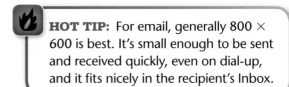 **HOT TIP:** For email, generally 800 × 600 is best. It's small enough to be sent and received quickly, even on dial-up, and it fits nicely in the recipient's Inbox.

? **DID YOU KNOW?**
The larger the image, the longer it will take to send and receive.

▶ **SEE ALSO:** Compose and send a new email in Chapter 9.

Print a picture

You can share a picture by printing it. Again, you can print from inside Photo Gallery.

1 Open Photo Gallery.

2 Select a picture to print. (You can also double-click the image as I've done here.)

3 Click Print.

4 Click Print again.

5 Using the Print Pictures wizard, select the type and number of prints to create.

6 Click Print.

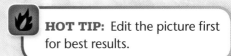

? DID YOU KNOW?
You can click Order prints online to get prints delivered to you using an online printing company.

🔥 HOT TIP: Edit the picture first for best results.

Add folders to Windows Live Photo Gallery

Photo Gallery looks for digital files in four places: My Pictures, Public Pictures, My Videos and Public Videos. If you've created your own folders outside of these four places and put pictures in them, you'll have to tell Photo Gallery where those folders are.

1 Open Windows Live Photo Gallery.

2 Click File, and click Include a Folder in the Gallery.

3 Expand the 'trees' to locate the folder to add.

4 Click OK.

5 Click OK in the dialogue box that appears.

> **? DID YOU KNOW?**
> Once added, a new folder will appear in the View pane.

> **? DID YOU KNOW?**
> It's best to keep all pictures in the Pictures folder, organised in subfolders you create.

Personalise Windows Live Photo Gallery

You can personalise Windows Live Photo Gallery quickly and easily. You can change the size of the picture thumbnails, what information is shown with the thumbnails, and more.

1 In Windows Live Photo Gallery, use the slider to change the size of the thumbnails.

2 Right-click an empty area of the interface, click View, and choose what else should be shown with the thumbnails.

3 Click Extras, and click Download more photo tools to get additional editing features.

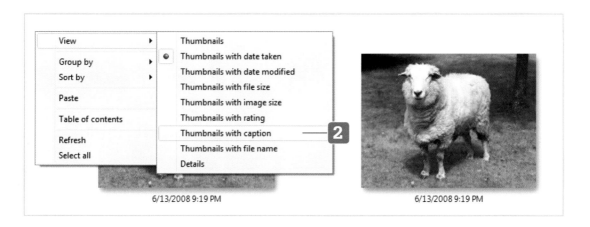

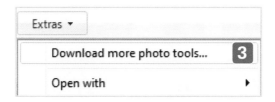

6 Windows Media Player

Introduction

If you like to listen to music or watch DVDs on your computer, Windows Media Player has everything you need. You can get music online, copy the CDs from your own music collection to your PC, and create favourite playlists of music you listen to often. You can also copy your favourite music to your own CDs to listen to in the car, share music with other users on your local network, and more. Unlike some programs that have to be downloaded, like Windows Live Photo Gallery, Windows Media Player is part of Windows 7 and requires no extra effort to obtain it.

Open Media Player and locate music

You open Media Player the same way you open other programs, from the Start menu. Once opened, you'll need to know where the Library button is, so you can access different kinds of media. We'll start with music.

1 Open Media Player from the taskbar.

2 Click the arrow next to the Library button.

3 Click Music. (This is really a moot point because Music is the default, but you need to know how to get here to switch to other media libraries.)

 ALERT: The first time you start Windows Media Player, you'll be prompted to set it up. Choose Express to accept the default settings.

WHAT DOES THIS MEAN?
Windows Media Player: an application included with Windows 7. You can watch DVDs and videos here, listen to and manage music, and even listen to radio stations or view pictures.

Listen to a song

To play any music track, simply navigate to it and double-click it. Songs are listed in the Navigation pane. *Navigate* is a fancy word for 'locate and click'.

1 Open Media Player. If necessary, click the Library button and choose Music.

2 Click Album. (Note you can also click Artist, Genre or any other category to locate a song.)

3 Double-click any album to play it.

4 Double-click any song on the album to play it.

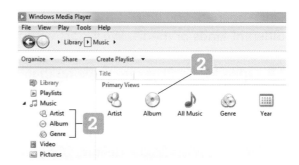

Double-click a song to play it

This line shows the song's progress

Controls

? DID YOU KNOW?

The controls at the bottom of the screen from left to right are: Shuffle (to play songs in random order), Repeat, Stop, Previous, Play/Pause, Next, Mute, and a volume slider. Use these controls to manage the music that's playing.

? DID YOU KNOW?

Media Player has Back and Forward buttons you can use to navigate Media Player.

Edit a song title and other information

Occasionally, the song title or album title won't be correct (or you remember it was once named something else or had various versions). You can edit any data relating to a song or album by right-clicking it.

1 In Media Player, locate the song or album title to change.

2 Right-click the song and click Edit.

3 Type a new title for the song or album.

4 Press Enter on the keyboard.

? DID YOU KNOW?

The list that appears after right-clicking an item is called the 'shortcut menu'.

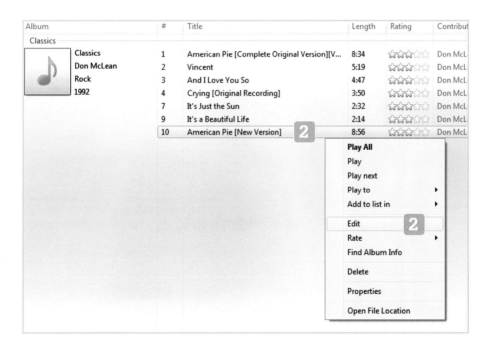

? DID YOU KNOW?

You can type whatever title you want, as shown here.

Copy a CD to your hard drive

You can copy CDs to your hard drive. This is called 'ripping'. To rip means to copy in media-speak. Once music is on your PC, you can listen to it in Media Player, burn compilations of music to other CDs, and even put the music on a portable music player.

1 Insert the CD to copy into the CD drive.

2 Deselect any songs you do not want to copy to your PC.

3 In Windows Media Player, click the Rip CD button.

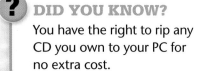

Rip progress

Copy files to a CD

There are two ways to take music with you when you are on the road or on the go. You can copy the music to a portable device like a music player or you can create your own CD, choosing the songs to copy and placing them on the CD in the desired order.

1 Open Media Player.

2 Insert a blank CD, and if necessary click the Burn tab.

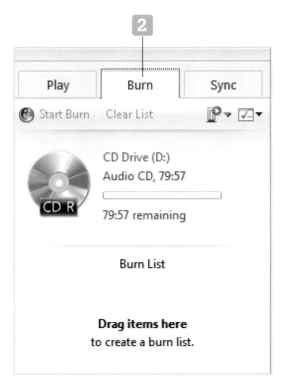

ALERT: A typical CD can hold about 80 minutes of music.

DID YOU KNOW?
CDs you create in Media Player can be played in car stereos and portable CD players, as well as lots of other CD devices.

DID YOU KNOW?
Media Player will keep track of the songs you select and will let you know when you're running out of space on the CD you are creating.

3 Click any song title or album to add, and drag it to the List pane. Look at the slider in the List pane to see how much room is left on the CD. Here there is just over 19 minutes left.

4 When you've added the songs you want, click Start Burn.

? **DID YOU KNOW?**

You can right-click any entry to access additional options including Remove from List, Move Up, or Move Down.

WHAT DOES THIS MEAN?

Burn: a term used to describe the process of copying music from a computer to a CD.

Watch a DVD

You can watch a DVD on your computer just as you would on any DVD player. Windows 7 offers two choices for doing so, Windows Media Center and Windows Media Player. We'll talk about Windows Media Player here.

1 Find the button on the PC's tower, keyboard or laptop that opens the DVD drive door. Press it.

2 Place the DVD in the door and press the button again to close it.

3 If prompted, choose to play the DVD movie using Windows Media Player. You probably will not be prompted.

 HOT TIP: To access controls to fast-forward, pause, rewind, or perform other tasks, move the mouse to the bottom of the screen.

 HOT TIP: The controls you'll see and use in Media Player are very similar to (and perhaps exactly like) the controls you see on your own DVD player.

Create a playlist

Playlists allow you to organise songs the way you like to listen to them. You might consider creating playlists that contain songs specific to an occasion, like a dinner party, after-pub party or similar event. Then, when the event happens, you can simply put on the playlist and let the music take care of itself.

1 Open Windows Media Player and click Create Playlist.

2 When you click Create Playlist, the type will turn blue. Type the name of the playlist here. (Note that the new playlist name will appear under Playlists.)

3 Locate any song or album to add to the playlist.

4 Drag (and drop) these to the new playlist, in this case Party Music.

5 Continue to drag and drop songs as desired.

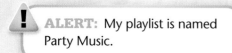

ALERT: My playlist is named Party Music.

DID YOU KNOW?
To play any playlist, double-click it in the Playlists pane in the Navigation window.

Share your Music Library

If you have more than one PC in your home and those PCs are networked, you can share your media library with them. Sharing allows you to keep only one copy of media (music, videos, pictures) on one PC, while sharing it with other PCs running Windows Media Player, various media extenders and Microsoft's Xbox 360.

1 Open Windows Media Player and click the Stream button.

2 Click Turn on media streaming. Click Turn on media streaming again, in the next window.

3 Review the sharing options.

4 Click OK.

HOT TIP: To receive media on this PC, click Receive media on your network.

HOT TIP: To tweak these settings to allow only specific devices to access media, repeat these steps and click Choose devices.

ALERT: The Windows 7 PC that stores the media you want to share must be connected to your home network. The network must be private.

Configure options

You may want to tweak the options available in Media Player. There are lots of options to consider, especially the ones related to privacy. There's not much to worry about though, not many hackers are going to want to hack into your PC via Media Player.

1 Open Media Player.

2 Click Tools, then Options. (If you can't see the Tools menu, click the Alt key on the keyboard.)

3 From the Options dialogue box, click Privacy.

4 Apply changes as desired.

5 When finished, click OK.

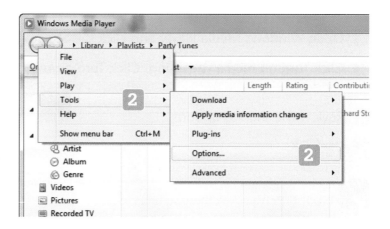

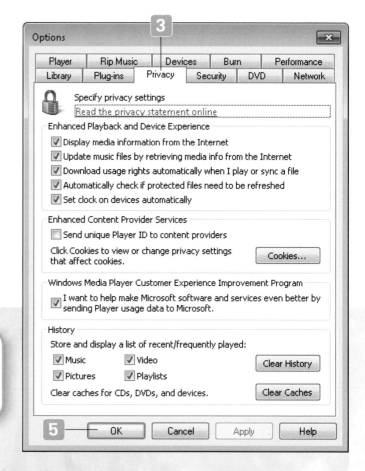

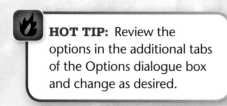

HOT TIP: Review the options in the additional tabs of the Options dialogue box and change as desired.

7 Windows Media Center

Introduction

Windows Media Center is included with the most popular versions of Windows 7. Media Center is a one-stop media application that lets you access and manage pictures, videos, movies, music, online media, television, DVDs and CDs, and radio.

You should start with Media Center by watching and recording TV, and then move on to watching DVDs and viewing online media. As time passes and you get more comfortable with Media Center, you may find you prefer it over Media Player and Photo Gallery for managing other media too.

Note: If you're retired and travel a lot, you can use Media Center to watch TV and other media when it would otherwise be unavailable. For instance, you can record your favourite shows while your laptop is docked at home, and then take the laptop with you when you travel. You'll always have something to watch!

Open Media Center

Think of all the things you'd need to watch TV and DVDs at home. Now think about what you'd need connected to (or installed in) your PC or laptop. You'll need speakers, a CD/DVD drive, and a TV tuner for best performance. You'll also need an Internet connection to watch Internet TV, access the Guide and download online media.

1 Click Start.

2 Click Windows Media Center.

ALERT: Not all computers come with a TV tuner. If your computer does not, you won't be able to watch live TV until you purchase and install one.

HOT TIP: Media Center's interface includes several menus: TV, Movies, Sports, Tasks, Extras, Pictures + Videos, and Music.

DID YOU KNOW?
You'll also find Media Center from Start and All Programs.

Set up Media Center

The first time you open Media Center, you'll be prompted to set it up. The easiest set-up is to choose Express.

1 Open Media Center.

2 When you see the set-up screen shown here, click Continue.

3 When prompted, click Express.

4 If you want to set up your TV signal, refer to the next section, Set up a TV signal.

HOT TIP: Make sure all the hardware you'll need is installed, connected and turned on before opening Media Center for the first time.

? DID YOU KNOW?
You can always configure hardware after this initial set-up if you add hardware later.

Set up a TV signal

To watch live TV, you have to tell Media Center how you connect to your TV signal (and your PC has to have a TV tuner). There are many ways to watch TV, including but not limited to using an antenna, using a cable box, making a connection directly from a coaxial connection in the wall, using a satellite dish, and more.

1 Use the arrow keys on the keyboard or remote control to locate TV and live tv setup.

2 Choose the options that apply to your TV set-up and connection. You may have to input a zip code (postcode), choose what type of connection you use, agree to some terms of service, and/or answer other questions regarding your television service.

3 As prompted, make the proper choices, working through the wizard. Click Finish when done.

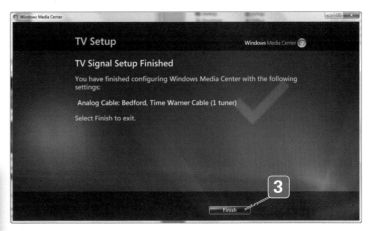

 HOT TIP: Once you record TV, you no longer have to be connected to your TV tuner. This means you can buy an external tuner if you like, and use it when you want.

ALERT: Because each option results in a personalised 'next step' when setting up your TV signal, it's not possible to work through each scenario here.

HOT TIP: Once the signal is set up, Windows Media Center will download information for up to 14 days of TV programming. You can use the results to record and watch television.

Watch, pause and rewind live TV

When you open Media Center, TV is the default option, and Recorded TV is selected. To watch live television, you'll need to use the mouse, keyboard, or remote control to move to the right, to live TV. While watching live TV, you can watch, pause and rewind the show (and fast forward through previously paused programming).

1 Open Media Center.

2 Move to the right of recorded TV and click live tv.

3 Position the mouse at the bottom of the live TV screen to show the controls.

4 Use the controls to manage live TV.

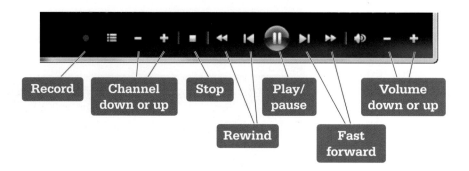

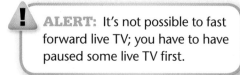

 ALERT: It's not possible to fast forward live TV; you have to have paused some live TV first.

HOT TIP: Press pause at the beginning of a 30-minute show for 10 minutes and you can fast forward through the commercials. (For a 60-minute show, pause for 20 minutes.)

 ALERT: If you receive an error when you click live tv, it's either because you do not have the television signal properly set up or you don't have a TV tuner.

Obtain programme information

When you're watching live TV, you'll see the broadcast, of course, but other items will appear and disappear, based on where you move the mouse. The show's broadcast information appears when you change to the channel, and you can also bring it up by right-clicking an area of the screen.

1 Open Media Center.

2 Under TV, click live tv.

3 Right-click at the bottom of the screen near the TV controls to access additional information about the show.

4 Hover the mouse over program info, details, zoom and captions (not shown, but you'll see it when you move the mouse to the right) to view additional information or to view captions.

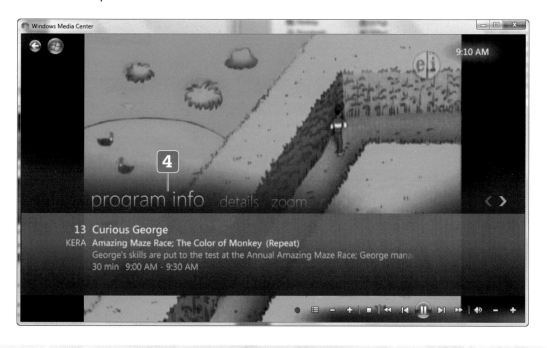

 HOT TIP: Click the right or left arrows for more information about the show, to turn on closed captioning, to see a synopsis of the show, and more.

 DID YOU KNOW?

Miss something? Drag the slider to the left to rewind live TV. When to stop watching TV? Click the square Stop button.

Record a future TV show

You can click the Record button while watching live TV to record the show you're watching. You won't always want to record what you're watching though; you will more likely want to record something that is coming on later in the week. That's what the Guide is for.

1 Open Media Center.

2 Under TV, move right and click Guide.

3 Locate a show to record.

4 Right-click the programme and click Record.

5 The programme will have a red dot on it in the Guide listings. Click it to configure additional settings or to view additional airings. (Use the arrow keys to access the information.)

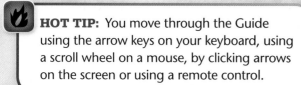

HOT TIP: You move through the Guide using the arrow keys on your keyboard, using a scroll wheel on a mouse, by clicking arrows on the screen or using a remote control.

 HOT TIP: Use the Back button to navigate through Media Center.

Record a future TV series

When you record a series, you record every show related to the series. You can tell Media Center to record all shows (including reruns) or just new ones, among other options.

1 Open Media Center.

2 Under TV, move right and click guide.

3 Locate a show to record.

4 Right-click the programme.

5 Click Record Series.

 HOT TIP: Record a series of shows you like or record a show your grandchildren like. Then you can watch them in your car, when travelling on a plane, or when you need a break from the family.

 HOT TIP: You move through the Guide using the arrow keys on your keyboard, using a scroll wheel on a mouse, by clicking arrows on the screen or using a remote control.

 ALERT: If another show is set to record during this time, you'll be alerted of a 'conflict' and will have to configure which of the conflicting programmes should record.

 HOT TIP: To cancel a recording, click the programme and click Do Not Record. To stop recording a series, click Series Info and Cancel Series.

Watch a recorded TV show

To watch a television show you've recorded, simply browse to TV, Recorded TV, and click the recorded show you want to watch!

1 Open Media Center, and under TV, click recorded tv.

2 Locate the programme to watch.

3 Click the show to watch, and click play.

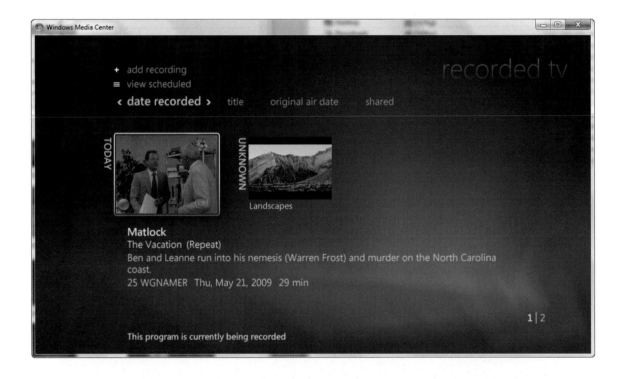

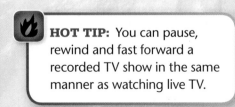 **HOT TIP:** You can pause, rewind and fast forward a recorded TV show in the same manner as watching live TV.

 **DID YOU KNOW?**
When you record a series, a folder will be created for it that will hold the related shows.

View your pictures

Although you can use Windows Live Photo Gallery to view your pictures, you may find you like Media Center better.

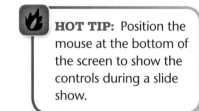

HOT TIP: Position the mouse at the bottom of the screen to show the controls during a slide show.

1 Open Media Center.

2 Scroll to Pictures + Videos, and click picture library.

3 Browse through the available pictures and picture folders.

4 Click play slide show to play a slide show of the pictures in that folder.

Watch a DVD

When you insert a DVD into your Windows 7 PC, by default it plays in Media Player. If you desire, you can also watch a DVD in Media Center.

1 Make sure Windows Media Center is open and put a DVD in the DVD drive.

2 If the DVD opens in Media Player, click the X to close Media Player.

3 In Windows Media Center, under Movies, select play dvd.

4 Use the mouse, remote control or arrow on the keyboard to play the movie, view special features or select other options.

5 Use the controls introduced earlier to pause, stop, rewind and fast forward through the movie.

Listen to music

You know you can listen to music in Media Player but you can also listen to music in Media Center.

1 Open Media Center.

2 Scroll to Music and click music library.

3 Locate the album to play. (You can also put a music CD in the CD drive.)

4 Click Play Album, or select any other option.

5 While the music is playing, click Visualize. This will allow you to 'see' the music with the computer's visual representation of it. Click the Back button to return to the screen shown here.

? DID YOU KNOW?

You can click artists, genres, songs, playlists, and more to refine the list.

? DID YOU KNOW?

Click Shuffle to play the songs on the album or playlist in random order.

Explore Internet TV

Under Extras, you'll find Internet TV. You can watch quite a few shows on Internet TV, provided you have a working Internet connection.

1 Open Media Center.

2 Click Extras, and select InternetTV.

3 Browse the offerings, and when you find something you like, click it to watch.

 HOT TIP: You'll want a broadband connection for best performance when watching Internet TV.

 HOT TIP: You may be able to choose from a list of shows after selecting an item in step 3.

8 Getting online

Introduction

If you don't yet have access to the Internet, it's time to get on board. These days, you are expected do certain things online, from making travel reservations to paying bills to communicating with friends and family. Of course, you can opt to do more, like shopping, researching or playing games, but increasingly you are *required* to have access. It's no longer a luxury!

You have a few things to do before you can get online though. You need to select an Internet Service Provider (ISP), call it and set up a service, and then select an email address and password. Finally, you'll have to write down the configuration settings the company will give you. Once you have all of that, you'll be ready to go.

There is one exception to subscribing to an ISP and paying for it monthly; you can visit free or minimal cost 'hotspots' where you can get online and with no configuration tasks, provided you have a wireless network adapter installed in your PC. If you have a new laptop, you probably do. If you have a desktop PC, you're probably out of luck though. Mind you, even if you do have a wireless network adapter, you're not going to want to lug your huge PC and a monitor to the local coffee shop just to get online.

Select an ISP and obtain the proper settings

There are several ways to choose an Internet Service Provider (ISP). Ask the younger generations what ISPs they use, and ask them for a recommendation. You may also be able to get a service from your mobile phone company. Call and ask around to find the best options and price. Call the company you've decided on and tell them that you want to set up a service. It's best to get broadband or cable, but it's also OK to opt for satellite.

There are some important things to ask the representative when you are setting up your service, and you must write these things down and keep them in a safe place. You'll be prompted to enter the information when you set up your email.

1 User name.

2 Email address.

3 Password.

4 Incoming POP3 server name.

5 Outgoing SMTP server name.

6 Display Name (may be the same as user name).

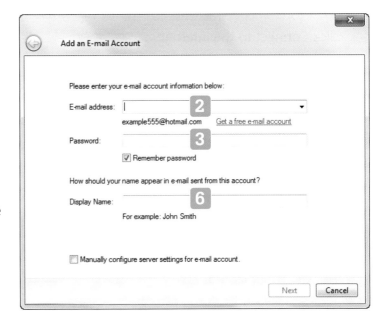

Add an E-mail Account

Please enter your e-mail account information below:

E-mail address: | 2
example555@hotmail.com   Get a free e-mail account

Password: 3
☑ Remember password

How should your name appear in e-mail sent from this account?

Display Name: 6
For example: John Smith

☐ Manually configure server settings for e-mail account.

Next   Cancel

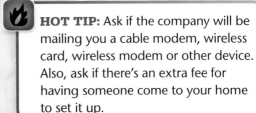

ALERT: You'll need this information to set up your email account and to log on to the Internet using your paid service.

HOT TIP: Ask if the company will be mailing you a cable modem, wireless card, wireless modem or other device. Also, ask if there's an extra fee for having someone come to your home to set it up.

Create a connection

Before you can connect to the Internet, you need to install any hardware you received from your provider. It should come with instructions and a help line phone number, and some providers will even come to your house and set up the hardware for you. Once the hardware is up and running, you can access the Network and Sharing Center to view and manage the connection.

1 Click Start.

2 In the Start Search window, type Network and Sharing.

3 Under Programs, select Network and Sharing Center.

4 Click Set up a new connection or network.

5 Click Connect to the Internet – Set up a wireless, broadband, or dial-up connection to the Internet. Click Next.

6 When prompted, enter the information you obtained from your ISP. This may include a user name and password.

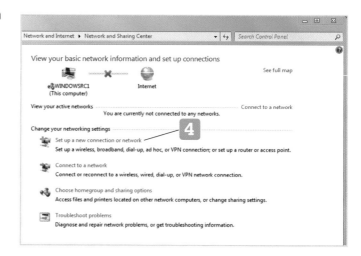

7 Continue until you've input all of the required information and click Connect.

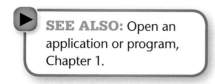

SEE ALSO: Open an application or program, Chapter 1.

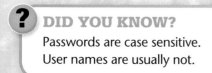

? DID YOU KNOW?

Passwords are case sensitive. User names are usually not.

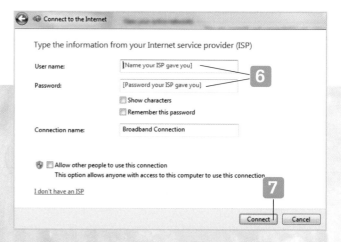

Diagnose connection problems

If you are having trouble connecting to the Internet, you can diagnose Internet problems using the Network and Sharing Center. However, if you have just installed new hardware, it is probably best to call your ISP for help first.

1 Open the Network and Sharing Center. If you are connected to the Internet, you will see a green line between your computer and the Internet. If you are not connected you will see a red x.

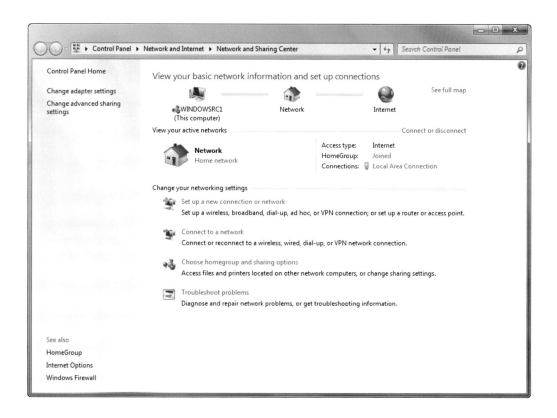

? DID YOU KNOW?

There are additional troubleshooting tips in the Help and Support pages. Click Start, and click Help and Support.

2 To diagnose a nonworking Internet connection, click the red x.

3 Take the suggested steps to resolve the problem. Note the troubleshooter here says the problem is indeed resolved after plugging in the network cable.

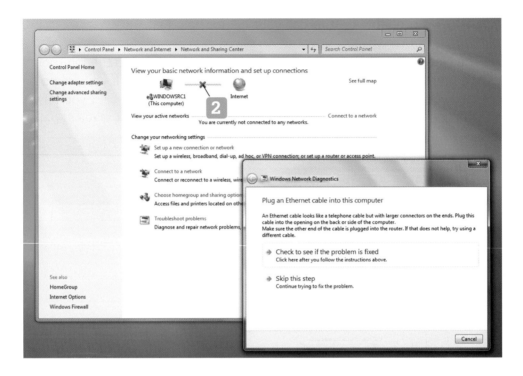

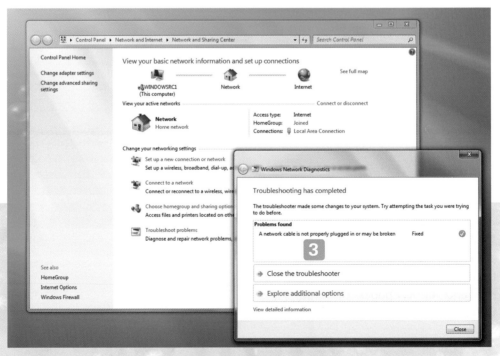

Join a network

When you connect a new PC running Windows 7 to a wired (Ethernet) network or get within range of a wireless one (and you have wireless hardware installed in your computer), Windows 7 will find the network and then ask you what kind of network it is. It's a public network if you're in a coffee shop, library or café, and it's a private network if it's a network you manage, like one already in your home.

1 Connect physically to a wired network using an Ethernet cable or, if you have wireless hardware installed in your laptop, get within range of a wireless network.

2 Select Home, Work or Public location. (If necessary input credentials.)

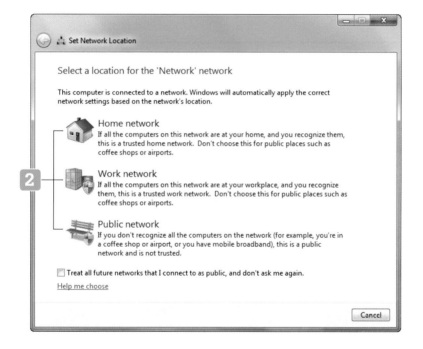

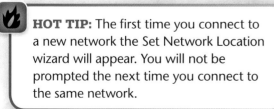

HOT TIP: The first time you connect to a new network the Set Network Location wizard will appear. You will not be prompted the next time you connect to the same network.

3 Click the Network icon in the Notification area of the taskbar to determine your connection status.

WHAT DOES THIS MEAN?

There are three network options, and when you see the Set Network Location dialogue box, you need to select one. Here's how to know which one to choose:

Home: choose this if the network is your home network or a network you trust (like a network at a friend's house). This connection type lets your computer *discover* other PCs, printers, and devices on the network, and they can see you.

Work: choose this if you are connecting to a network at work. The settings for Work and Home are the same, only the titles differ so you can tell them apart easily.

Public: choose this if the network you want to connect to is open to anyone within range of it, like networks in coffee shops, airports and libraries. Windows 7 assumes that if you choose Public, you only want to connect to the Internet and nothing else. It closes down *discoverability*, so that even your shared data is safe.

 DID YOU KNOW?

Connecting to an existing network allows you to access shared features of the network. In a coffee shop that's probably only a connection to the Internet; if it's a home network, it's your personal, shared data (and probably a connection to the Internet too).

Check for a wireless network card

If you have a laptop and don't want to pay for an Internet service, you can take your laptop to a 'free Internet hotspot' and connect to the Internet at no cost. However, your laptop must have the required wireless hardware. Specifically, you need a built-in wireless card (or a wireless adapter). You can find out if you have this hardware using Device Manager.

1 Click Start.

2 In the Start Search dialogue box, type Device Manager.

3 Under Programs, click Device Manager to open it.

4 Locate Network adapters. (Wireless hardware is called network adapters.)

5 Click the triangle to expand it: the triangle will appear sideways after you click it.

6 Look for a device with the word 'wireless' in it. If you do not see a wireless adapter listed, you do not have wireless capabilities.

7 Click the X in the top right corner of Device Manager to close it.

? DID YOU KNOW?

Even if you have no adapters, you can purchase a USB converter to obtain satellite Internet or a modem to use dial-up. There's always a way to get online!

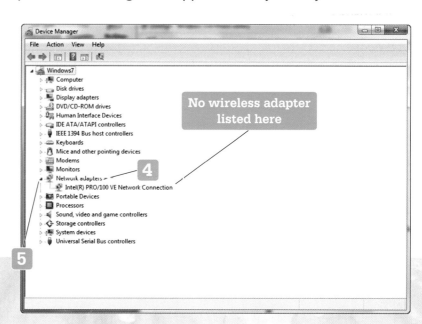

No wireless adapter listed here

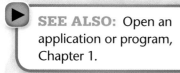

SEE ALSO: Open an application or program, Chapter 1.

Connect to a free hotspot

Wi-Fi hotspots are popping up all over the country in coffee houses, parks, libraries and more. Wi-Fi hotspots let you connect to the Internet without having to be tethered to an Ethernet cable or tied down with a high monthly wireless bill. You may have to buy a cup of coffee for the privilege, but hey, you were going to anyway, right?

1 Turn on your wireless laptop within range of a free hotspot. You'll be prompted that wireless networks are available.

2 If you see the wireless network you want to connect to in the pop-up, click it. If not, click the network icon in the Notification area of the taskbar to view all of the available wireless networks.

3 Click the network to connect to. You may be connected automatically.

4 If prompted, type the network security key. Click OK.

5 Click the icon in the Notification area of the taskbar to verify the connection has been made.

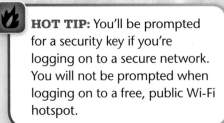

HOT TIP: You'll be prompted for a security key if you're logging on to a secure network. You will not be prompted when logging on to a free, public Wi-Fi hotspot.

ALERT: You'll need a laptop with the required wireless hardware to use a free hotspot.

HOT TIP: To find a Wi-Fi hotspot close to you, go to www.maps.google.com.uk and search for Wi-Fi hotspots.

Open a website in Internet Explorer

Windows 7 comes with Internet Explorer (IE), an application you can use to surf the Internet. Internet Explorer is a 'web browser', and it has everything you need, including a pop-up blocker, zoom settings, and the ability to save your favourite webpages. You'll use Internet Explorer to surf the Internet.

1 Open Internet Explorer from the taskbar. It's a big, blue E. A website will probably open automatically.

2 To go to a website you want to visit, type the name of the website in the window at the top of the page. This is called the address bar.

3 Press Enter on the keyboard.

 HOT TIP: You can also drag your mouse across an open website name to select it. Do not drag your mouse over the http://www part of the address and you won't have to retype it.

 HOT TIP: Every webpage contains a link to another webpage. Click the links to move from one page to another on the Internet.

WHAT DOES THIS MEAN?
Address bar: used to type in Internet addresses, also known as URLs (universal resource locators). Generally, an Internet address takes the form of http://www.*companyname*.com.

 ALERT: Websites almost always start with http://www.

Open a website in a new tab

You can open more than one website at a time in Internet Explorer. You might open one tab for your son's Facebook page, one for the BBC website and another for Google. To do this, click the tab that appears to the right of the open webpage. Then, type the name of the website you'd like to visit.

1 Open Internet Explorer.

2 Click an empty tab. An empty page will appear, with New Tab as its title.

3 Type the name of the website you'd like to visit in the address bar.

4 Press Enter on the keyboard.

HOT TIP: Type the following:
http://www.microsoft.com/uk

? DID YOU KNOW?

When a website name starts with https://, it means it's secure. When purchasing items online, make sure the payment pages have this prefix.

WHAT DOES THIS MEAN?

The Internet Explorer interface has several distinct parts.

Command bar: used to access icons such as the Home and Print icons.
Tabs: used to access websites when multiple sites are open.
Search window: used to search for anything on the Internet.

Set a home page

If you want specific pages to open every time you open Internet Explorer, you need to configure 'home' pages. You can select a single webpage or multiple webpages to be displayed each time you open IE. In fact, there are three options for configuring home pages:

- Use this webpage as your only home page – select this option if you only want one page to serve as your home page.
- Add this webpage to your home page tabs – select this option if you want this page to be one of several home pages.
- Use the current tab set as your home page – select this option if you've opened multiple tabs and you want all of them to be home pages.

1 Use the address bar to locate a webpage you want to use as your home page.

2 Click the arrow next to the Home icon.

3 Click Add or Change Home Page.

4 Make a selection using the information provided regarding each option.

5 Click Yes.

6 Repeat these steps as desired.

SEE ALSO: Open a website in Internet Explorer, earlier in this chapter.

ALERT: You have to locate the webpage before you can assign it as a home page.

HOT TIP: To open your home pages, click the Home icon on the toolbar.

Mark a favourite

Favourites are websites you save links to for accessing more easily at a later time. They differ from home pages because, by default, they do not open when you start Internet Explorer. The favourites you save appear in the Favorites Center and on the Favorites bar. You may see some favourites listed that you did not create, including Microsoft Websites and MSN Websites. Every time you save a favourite, it will appear in both places.

1 Go to the webpage you want to configure as a favourite.

2 Click the Add to Favorites icon.

3 Note the new icon for the favourite on the Favorites bar.

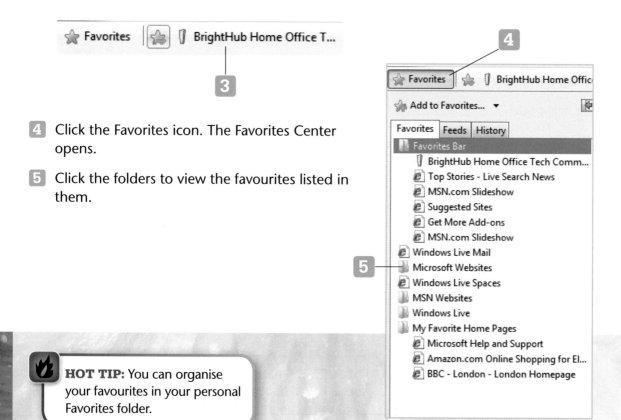

4 Click the Favorites icon. The Favorites Center opens.

5 Click the folders to view the favourites listed in them.

HOT TIP: You can organise your favourites in your personal Favorites folder.

Change the zoom level of a webpage

If your over 50s eyes give you trouble reading what's on a webpage because the text is too small, use the Page Zoom feature. Page Zoom works by preserving the fundamental design of the webpage you're viewing. This means that Page Zoom intelligently zooms in on the entire page, which maintains the page's integrity, layout and look.

1 Open Internet Explorer and browse to a webpage.

2 Click the arrow located at the bottom right of Internet Explorer to show the Zoom options.

3 Click 150%.

4 Notice how the webpage text and images increase. Use the scroll bars to navigate the page.

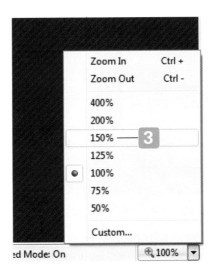

<table>
<tr><td>Zoom In</td><td>Ctrl +</td></tr>
<tr><td>Zoom Out</td><td>Ctrl -</td></tr>
<tr><td>400%</td><td></td></tr>
<tr><td>200%</td><td></td></tr>
<tr><td>150% ——3</td><td></td></tr>
<tr><td>125%</td><td></td></tr>
<tr><td>● 100%</td><td></td></tr>
<tr><td>75%</td><td></td></tr>
<tr><td>50%</td><td></td></tr>
<tr><td>Custom...</td><td></td></tr>
</table>

ed Mode: On   🔍 100% ▼

❓ DID YOU KNOW?

The term 'browse' is used to describe both locating a file on your hard drive and locating something on the Internet.

❓ DID YOU KNOW?

The Page Zoom options are located under the Page icon on the Command bar, under Zoom, but it's much easier to use the link at the bottom right of the browser window, on the Status bar.

Print a webpage

To print a webpage, simply click the Print icon on the Command bar. You can print funny emails for your friends who don't yet have Internet access or aren't as computer savvy as you are!

1 Open Internet Explorer and browse to a webpage.

2 Click the Print icon to print the page with no further input. To view print options, click the arrow to the right of the Print icon, as shown here.

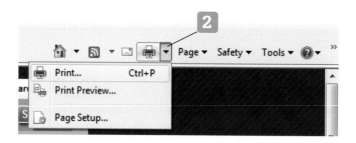

? DID YOU KNOW?

You can use the Snipping tool (Chapter 3) to take a screenshot of a webpage, and then you can write notes on it, email it or save it.

WHAT DOES THIS MEAN?

There are three menu options under the Print icon:

Print: clicking Print opens the Print dialogue box where you can configure the page range, select a printer, change page orientation, change print order and choose a paper type. Additional options include print quality, output bins and more. Of course, the choices offered depend on what your printer offers. If your printer can only print at 300×300 dots per inch, you can't configure it to print at a higher quality.

Print Preview: clicking Print Preview opens a window where you can see before you print what the print-out will actually look like. You can switch between portrait and landscape views, access the Page Setup dialogue box, and more.

Page Setup: clicking Page Setup opens the Page Setup dialogue box. Here you can select a paper size and source, and create headers and footers. You can also change orientation and margins, all of which are dependent on what features your printer supports.

Clear history

If you don't want people to be able to snoop around on your computer and find out what sites you've been visiting you'll need to delete your 'browsing history'. Deleting your browsing history lets you remove the information stored on your computer related to your Internet activities, like where you recently shopped and what you purchased.

1 Open Internet Explorer.

2 Click the Alt key on the keyboard if you do not see the menu shown here.

3 Click Tools.

4 Click Delete Browsing History. Note that you can also click Safety and select Delete Browsing History.

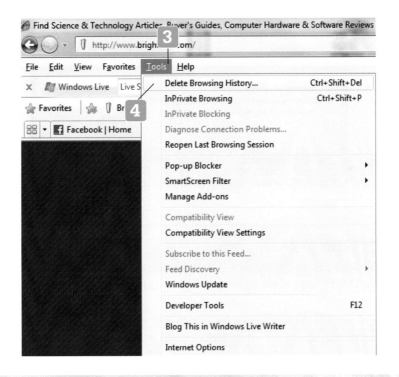

ALERT: Clicking the Alt key on the keyboard is what causes the Menu bar to appear.

5 To delete any or all of the listed items after selecting them, click the Delete button.

6 Click Close when finished.

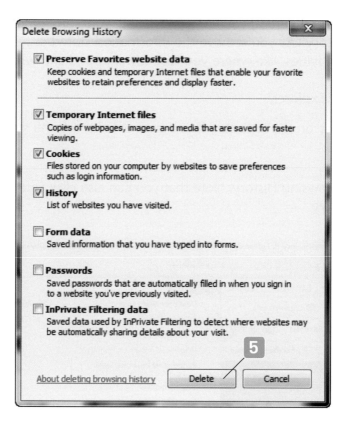

WHAT DOES THIS MEAN?

Temporary Internet files: these are files that have been downloaded and saved in your Temporary Internet files folder. A snooper could go through these files to see what you've been doing online.

Cookies: these are small text files that include data that identifies your preferences when you visit particular websites. Cookies are what allow you to visit, say, www.amazon.com and be greeted with Hello <your name>, We have recommendations for you! Cookies help a site offer you a personalised web experience.

History: this is the list of websites you've visited and any web addresses you've typed. Anyone can look at your History list to see where you've been.

Form data: information that's been saved using Internet Explorer's autocomplete form data functionality. If you don't want forms to be filled out automatically by you or someone else who has access to your PC and user account, delete this.

InPrivate Blocking data: data that was saved by InPrivate Blocking to detect where websites may be automatically sharing details about your visit.

Stay safe online

There's a chapter in this book on security, Chapter 10. In it, you'll learn how to use Windows Firewall, Windows Defender and other Security Center features. However, much of staying secure when online and surfing the Internet has more to do with common sense. When you're online, make sure to follow the guidelines listed here.

1 If you are connecting to a public network, make sure you select Public when prompted by Windows 7.

2 Always keep your PC secure with anti-virus software.

3 Limit the amount of confidential information you store on the Internet.

4 When making credit card purchases or travel reservations, always make sure the website address starts with https://.

5 Always sign out of any secure website you enter.

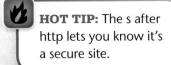

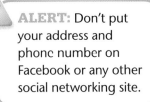

? DID YOU KNOW?
When you connect to a network you know, like a network in your home, you select Home (or Work).

! ALERT: Don't put your address and phone number on Facebook or any other social networking site.

! ALERT: You have to purchase and install your own anti-virus software; it does not come with Windows 7.

🔥 HOT TIP: The s after http lets you know it's a secure site.

WHAT DOES THIS MEAN?

Domain name: for our use here, a domain name is synonymous with a website name.

Favourite: a webpage that you've chosen to maintain a shortcut for in the Favorites Center.

Home page: the webpage that opens when you open Internet Explorer. You can set the home page and configure additional pages to open as well.

Link: a shortcut to a webpage. Links are often offered in an email, document or webpage to allow you to access a site without having actually to type in its name. In almost all instances, links are underlined and in a different colour than the page they are configured on.

Load: a webpage must 'load' before you can access it. Some pages load instantly while others take a few seconds.

Navigate: the process of moving from one webpage to another or viewing items on a single webpage. Often the term is used as follows: 'Click the link to navigate to the new web page'.

Search: a term used when you type a word or group of words into a Search window. Searching for data produces results.

Scroll Up and Scroll Down: a process of using the scroll bars on a webpage or the arrow keys on a keyboard to move up and down the pages of a website.

Website: a group of webpages that contains related information. Microsoft's website contains information about Microsoft products, for instance.

URL: the information you type to access a website, like http://www.microsoft.com.

9 Working with email

Introduction

Although there are several options for setting up, retrieving and managing your email, my favourite option is to use a free program called Windows Live Mail. With Windows Live Mail you can view, send and receive email, manage your contacts, and manage sent, saved and incoming email. Within the Windows Live Mail interface you can also print email, create folders for storing email you want to keep, manage unwanted email, open attachments, send pictures inside an email, and more.

When setting up Windows Live Mail you need to know your email address, password and two email server addresses, all of which you can get from your ISP. In fact, you probably have this information if you worked through Chapter 8, Getting online. Then, you'll work through the simple wizard boxes, inputting the required information when prompted, to set up the program. Once Mail is set up, you're ready to send and receive mail. Don't worry, it's easy!

Note: Previous versions of Windows operating systems, like Windows XP and Windows 7, came with an email program already built in. That's not the case with Windows 7; you have to download and install a program yourself.

Download and install Windows Live Mail

Windows 7 does not come with its own email program. You have to obtain one yourself. The one you'll learn about in this chapter is Windows Live Mail. It's free, easy to obtain and install, and offers a wizard to help you set it up with your email information. If you've never downloaded and/or installed a program before, don't worry, it's really simple!

1 Open Internet Explorer and go to http://www.windowslive.com/mail.

2 Look for the Download now button and click it. You'll be prompted to click Download now once more on the next screen.

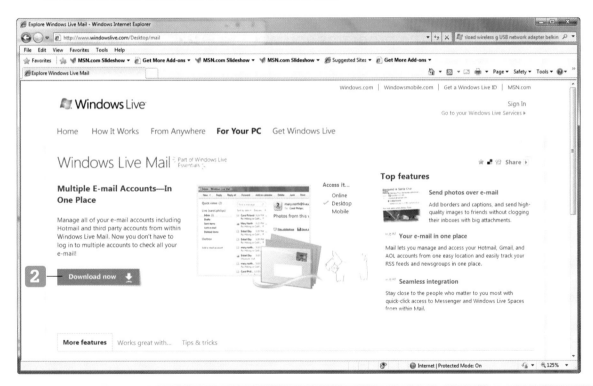

? DID YOU KNOW?

Your ISP may offer a place where you can get your email online without installing additional software; however, Windows Live Mail is probably much better than what it offers and is much more functional.

3 Click Run, and when prompted, click Yes.

4 Select the items to download. You can select all of the items, some of the items or only Mail, and then click Install.

5 When prompted to select your settings, make the desired choices. You can't go wrong here; there are no bad options.

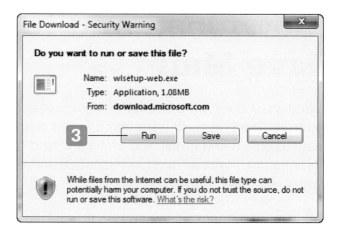

File Download - Security Warning

Do you want to run or save this file?

Name: wlsetup-web.exe
Type: Application, 1.08MB
From: **download.microsoft.com**

3 ── Run   Save   Cancel

While files from the Internet can be useful, this file type can potentially harm your computer. If you do not trust the source, do not run or save this software. What's the risk?

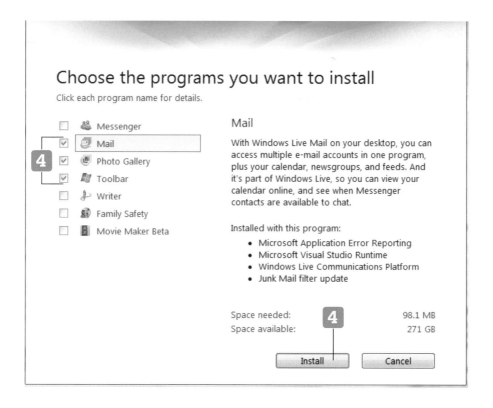

Choose the programs you want to install

Click each program name for details.

☐ 👥 Messenger
☑ 📧 Mail
4 ☑ 🖼 Photo Gallery
☑ 📊 Toolbar
☐ ✒ Writer
☐ 👪 Family Safety
☐ 🎬 Movie Maker Beta

Mail

With Windows Live Mail on your desktop, you can access multiple e-mail accounts in one program, plus your calendar, newsgroups, and feeds. And it's part of Windows Live, so you can view your calendar online, and see when Messenger contacts are available to chat.

Installed with this program:

- Microsoft Application Error Reporting
- Microsoft Visual Studio Runtime
- Windows Live Communications Platform
- Junk Mail filter update

Space needed: 4   98.1 MB
Space available: 271 GB

Install   Cancel

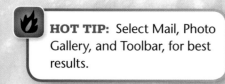

HOT TIP: Select Mail, Photo Gallery, and Toolbar, for best results.

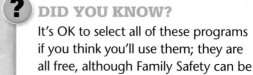

? DID YOU KNOW?

It's OK to select all of these programs if you think you'll use them; they are all free, although Family Safety can be a bit annoying if you don't need it.

Get a Windows Live account

When you use 'Live' services, like Windows Live Mail, Windows Live Photo Gallery, and others, you have to log into them using a Windows Live account. This account is free, and you can use it to sign into Live-related websites on the Internet. You need a Windows Live account. A Windows Live account is an email address and password you use to log into your Live programs on the Internet.

1 If you do not already have a Windows Live account, click Sign up after the installation of Live Mail completes. (You can also go to http://signup.live.com.)

2 Fill out the required information and click I accept when finished.

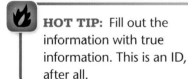

HOT TIP: Fill out the information with true information. This is an ID, after all.

DID YOU KNOW?

You can use your Windows Live email account as a regular email address, or simply use it to log into Live services on the Internet.

Set up a Windows Live email account in Mail

The first time you open Windows Live Mail you'll be prompted to input the required information regarding your email address and email servers. That's because Windows Live Mail is a program for sending and receiving email, and you can't do that without inputting the proper information. The easiest email account to set up is the one configured in the previous section, Get a Windows Live account. That's what you'll do here.

1 Open Windows Live Mail.

2 Click Add e-mail account.

2 ——— Add e-mail account

3 Type your Windows Live email account, password and display name.

4 If desired, leave Remember password ticked. Click Next.

5 Click Finish, and if prompted, click Download Now to retrieve your email.

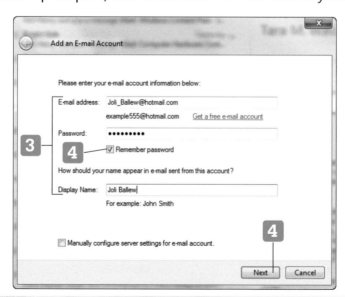

? **DID YOU KNOW?**
Your email address often takes this form: *yourname@yourispname.com*. Your display name can be anything you like.

? **DID YOU KNOW?**
Your display name is the name that will appear in the From field when you compose an email, and in the sender's inbox (under From in their email list) when someone receives email from you.

Set up a third-party email account

When you set up a Windows Live email account, Windows Live knows what settings to use and configure in the background. If you want to set up a third-party email account, you have to enter the settings manually. You get the information you need from your ISP.

1 Open Mail, and click Add e-mail account as detailed in the previous section.

2 Input your email address, password and display name.

3 When prompted, fill in the information for your incoming and outgoing mail servers. Click Next.

4 Click Finish.

? DID YOU KNOW?
Popular ISPs include Virgin, BT and AOL.

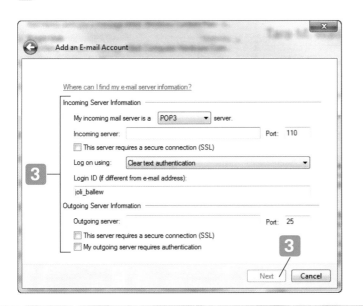

ALERT: You must input exactly what your ISP tells you to input! When in doubt, call the ISP or check its website for the proper settings.

ALERT: If your ISP told you your outgoing server requires authentication, tick the box. If you aren't sure, don't tick it.

HOT TIP: To resolve errors, click Tools, click Accounts, click the email account to change, and click Properties. You can then make changes to the mail servers, passwords and other settings.

View an email

Windows Live Mail checks for email automatically when you first open the program and every 30 minutes thereafter. If you want to check for email manually, you can click the Sync button any time you want. When you receive mail, there are two ways to read it. You can click the message once and read it in the Mail window, or double-click it to open it in its own window. I think it's best simply to click the email once; that way you don't have multiple open windows to deal with.

1 Click the Sync button.

2 Click the email once.

3 View the contents of the email.

ALERT: Email is received in the Inbox or the Unread e-mail box. If one of these is not selected, you must select it first!

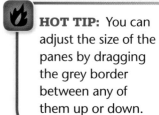

HOT TIP: You can adjust the size of the panes by dragging the grey border between any of them up or down.

WHAT DOES THIS MEAN?

Inbox: this folder holds mail you've received.

Outbox: this folder holds mail you've written but have not yet sent.

Sent items: this folder stores copies of messages you've sent.

Deleted items: this folder holds mail you've deleted.

Drafts: this folder holds messages you've started and saved, but not completed. Click File and click Save to put an email in progress here.

Junk e-mail: this folder holds email that Windows Live Mail thinks is spam. You should check this folder occasionally, since Mail may put email in there you want to read.

Unread e-mail: this folder shows email you have yet to read. Note there is one that contains email from contacts too, which only shows email from contacts in your address book.

Change how often Mail checks for email

You may want to have Mail check for email more or less often than every 30 minutes. It's easy to make the change.

1 Click Tools.

2 Click Options.

3 Click the General tab.

4 Change the number of minutes from 30 to something else.

5 Click OK.

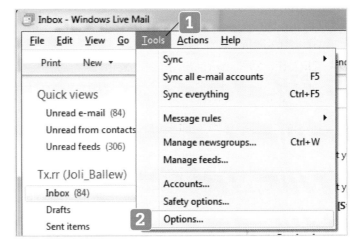

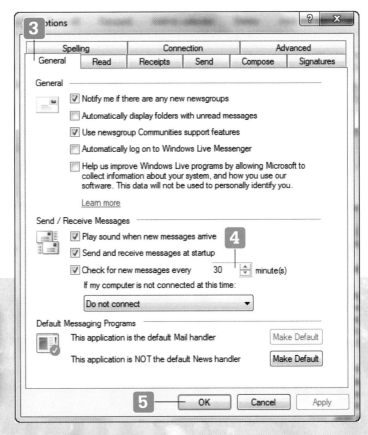

DID YOU KNOW?

You can change other settings in Mail from the other tabs in the Options dialogue box.

View an attachment

An attachment is a file that you can send with an email like a picture, document, video clip or something similar. If an email you receive contains an attachment, you'll see a paperclip. To open the attachment, click the paperclip icon in the Preview pane, and click the attachment's name.

1 Locate the paperclip icon in the Message pane and click it once.

2 Click Open.

> **ALERT:** Hackers send attachments that look as if they are from legitimate companies, banks and online services. Do not open these. Companies rarely send email attachments.

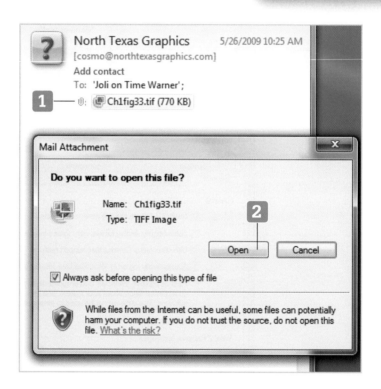

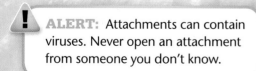

ALERT: Attachments can contain viruses. Never open an attachment from someone you don't know.

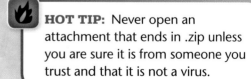

HOT TIP: Never open an attachment that ends in .zip unless you are sure it is from someone you trust and that it is not a virus.

Recover email from the Junk e-mail folder

Windows Live Mail has a junk email filter and anything it thinks is spam gets sent there. (Spam is another word for junk email.) Unfortunately, sometimes email gets sent to the Junk e-mail folder that is actually legitimate email. Therefore, once a week or so you should look in this folder to see if any email you want to keep is in there.

1 Click the Junk e-mail folder once.

2 Use the scroll bars if necessary to browse through the email in the folder.

3 If you see an email that is legitimate, click it once.

4 Click Not junk.

5 After reviewing the files, click Inbox.

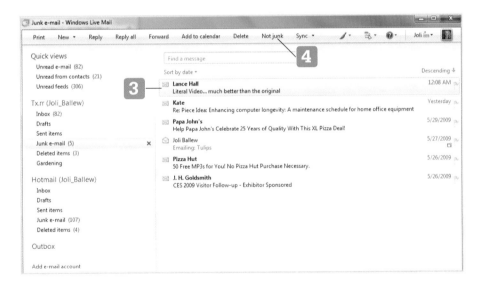

HOT TIP: When you tell Mail that a certain email is 'not junk', it remembers and should not flag email from this sender as spam again.

HOT TIP: When you click Not junk, the email is sent to your Inbox folder.

ALERT: Mail requires routine maintenance including deleting email from the Junk e-mail folder, among others. You'll learn how to delete items in a folder later in this chapter.

Reply to an email

When someone sends you an email, you may need to send a reply back to them. You do that by selecting the email and then clicking the Reply button.

1 Select the email you want to reply to in the Message pane.

2 Click Reply.

3 Type the message in the body pane.

4 Click Send.

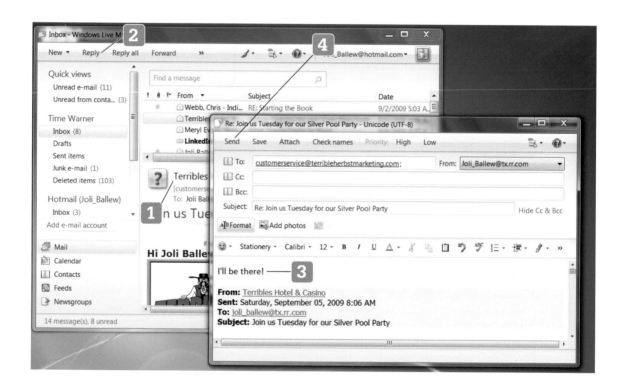

 **HOT TIP:** Mail offers formatting tools that you can use to change the font, font colour, font size, and more.

! ALERT: If the email you are replying to was sent to you along with additional people, clicking Reply will send a reply to the person who composed the message. Clicking Reply all will send the reply to everyone who received the email.

Forward an email

When someone sends you an email that you want to share with others, you forward the email. You do that by selecting the email and then clicking the Forward button.

1 Select the email you want to forward in the Message pane.

2 Click Forward.

3 In the To field, type the email address for the recipient.

4 Type a subject in the Subject field.

5 Type the message in the body pane.

6 Click Send.

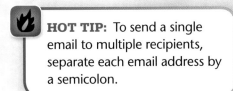

HOT TIP: To send a single email to multiple recipients, separate each email address by a semicolon.

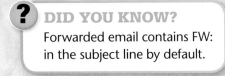

DID YOU KNOW?
Forwarded email contains FW: in the subject line by default.

Compose and send a new email

You compose an email message by clicking New on the toolbar. You input who the email should be sent to, the subject, and then you type the message.

1 Click New.

2 Type the recipient's email address in the To line. If you want to add additional names, separate each email address by a semicolon.

3 Type a subject in the Subject field.

4 Type the message in the body pane.

5 Click Send.

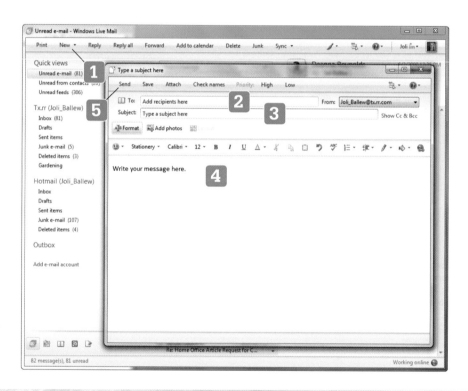

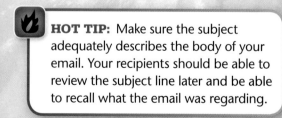

HOT TIP: Make sure the subject adequately describes the body of your email. Your recipients should be able to review the subject line later and be able to recall what the email was regarding.

DID YOU KNOW?

When working with email, make sure Mail is selected in the bottom left corner of the Live Mail Window. Other options include Calendar, Contacts, Feeds and Newsgroups.

If you want to send the email to someone and you don't need them to respond, you can put them in the Cc line.

If you want to send the email to someone and you don't want other recipients to know you included the individual in the email, add the individual's address to the Bcc line. You can show this by clicking Show Cc and Bcc.

WHAT DOES THIS MEAN?

Cc: stands for carbon copy.

Bcc: stands for blind carbon copy and is a secret copy.

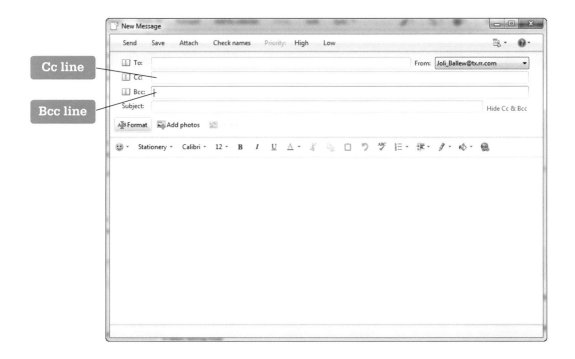

Cc line

Bcc line

HOT TIP: Select Tools, and click Select from contacts to add email addresses from your address book.

Attach a picture to an email using Attach

Although email that contains only a message serves its purpose quite a bit of the time, often you'll want to send a photograph, a short video, a sound recording, a document or other data. When you want to add something to your message other than text, it's called adding an attachment. There are many ways to attach something to an email.

1 Click New.

2 Click Attach.

3 Browse to the location of the file to attach.

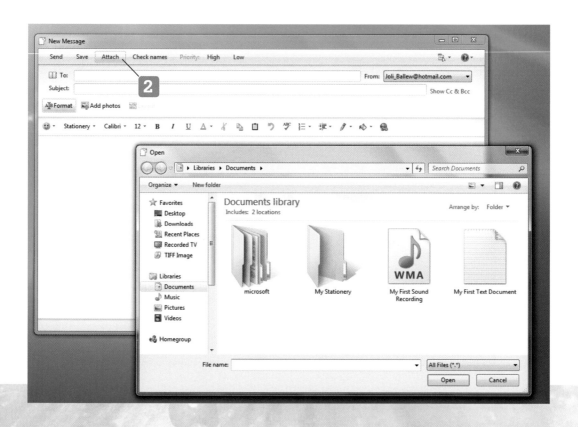

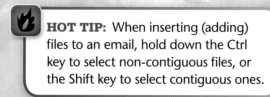

HOT TIP: When inserting (adding) files to an email, hold down the Ctrl key to select non-contiguous files, or the Shift key to select contiguous ones.

4 Select the file and click Open.

5 Complete the email message and click Send.

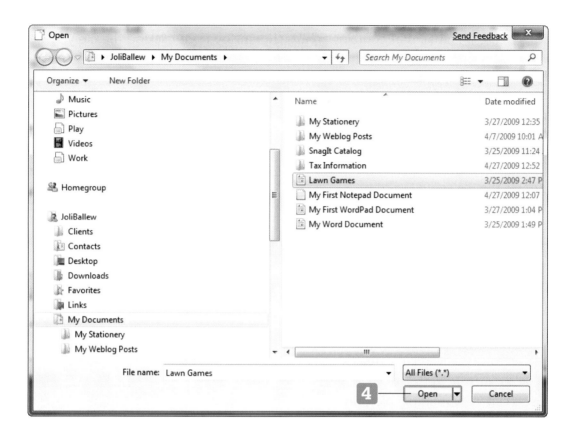

Attach a picture to an email using a right-click

You can create an email that contains an attachment by right-clicking the file you want to attach. This method attaches the files to a new email, which is fine if you want to create a new email. The only problem with this is that it doesn't work if you'd rather send forwards or replies. However, this method has a feature other methods don't. With it, you can resize any images you've selected before sending them. This is a great perk because many pictures are too large to send via email, and resizing them helps manage an email's size.

1 Locate the file you'd like to attach and right-click it.

2 Point to Send to.

3 Click Mail recipient.

4 If the item you're attaching is a picture, choose the picture size.

5 If prompted to send a photo email, click Yes. You'll be able to edit the picture in the email and users can view multiple pictures as a slide show.

? **DID YOU KNOW?**
800 × 600 is usually the best option when sending pictures via email.

? **DID YOU KNOW?**
You can email from within applications, such as Microsoft Word or Excel. Generally, you'll find the desired option under the File menu, as a submenu of Send.

! **ALERT:** Avoid sending large attachments, especially to people you know have a dial-up modem or those who get email only on a small device like a BlackBerry, iPhone or Mobile PC.

Add a contact

A contact is a data file that holds the information you keep about a person. The contact information looks like a 'contact card', and the information can include a picture, email address, mailing address, first and last name, and similar data. You obtain contacts from various sources: people you email, people you instant message with Windows Live Messenger, and more.

1 From Windows Live Mail, click Contacts. Mail is the default.

2 Click New.

3 Type all of the information you want to add. Be sure to add information to each tab.

4 Click Add contact.

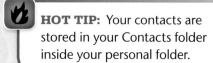

? DID YOU KNOW?

When someone gives you their email address and other personal data, you can create a contact card for them. From the File menu, select New, and then select Contact.

🔥 HOT TIP: Your contacts are stored in your Contacts folder inside your personal folder.

Print an email

Sometimes you'll need to print an email or its attachment. Windows Live Mail makes it easy to print. Just click Print on the toolbar. After clicking Print, the Print dialogue box will appear where you can select a printer, set print preferences, choose a page range, and well, print.

1 Select the email to print by clicking it in the Message pane.

2 Click File, and Print.

3 In the Print dialogue box, select the printer to use, if more than one exists.

4 Click Print.

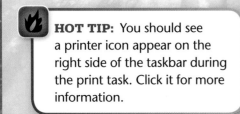 **HOT TIP:** You should see a printer icon appear on the right side of the taskbar during the print task. Click it for more information.

? DID YOU KNOW?
You can configure print preferences and choose what pages to print using Preferences. Refer to your printer's user manual to find out what print options your printer supports.

Apply a junk mail filter

Just like you receive unwanted information from estate agents, radio stations and television ads, you're going to get unwanted advertisements in emails. This is referred to as junk email or spam. Most of these advertisements are scams and rip-offs, and they often contain pornographic images. There are four filtering options in Windows Live Mail: No automatic filtering, Low, High, and Safe List Only.

1 Click Tools.

2 Click Junk E-mail, and click Safety options.

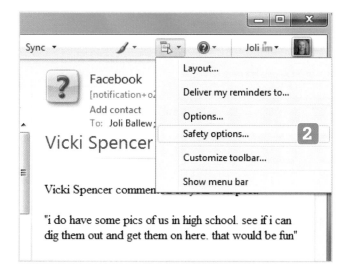

3 From the Options tab, make a selection.

4 Click the Phishing tab.

5 Select Protect my Inbox from messages with potential Phishing links. Additionally, move phishing email to the Junk e-mail folder.

6 Click OK.

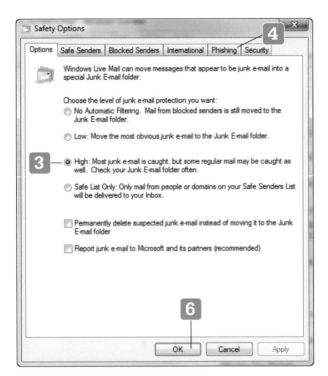

ALERT: Check the junk email folder often to make sure no legitimate email has been moved there.

SEE ALSO: Recover email from the Junk e-mail folder, earlier in this chapter.

WHAT DOES THIS MEAN?

No Automatic Filtering: use this only if you do not want Windows Live Mail to block junk email messages. Windows Live Mail will continue to block messages from email addresses listed on the Blocked Senders list.

Low: use this option if you receive very little junk email. You can start here and increase the filter if it becomes necessary.

High: use this option if you receive a lot of junk email and want to block as much of it as possible. Use this option for children's email accounts. Note that some valid email will probably be blocked, so you'll have to review the Junk e-mail folder occasionally, to make sure you aren't missing any email you want to keep.

Safe List Only: use this option if you only want to receive messages from people or domain names on your Safe Senders list. This is a drastic step, and requires you to add every sender you want to receive mail from to the Safe Senders list. Use this as a last resort.

Create a folder

It's important to perform some housekeeping chores once a month or so. If you don't, Windows Live Mail may become bogged down and perform more slowly than it should, or you may be unable to manage the email you want to keep. One way you can keep Mail under control is to create a new folder to hold email you want to keep and move mail into it.

1 Click the arrow next to New, and click Folder.

2 Type a name for the new folder.

3 Select a parent folder. The folder you create will appear underneath it.

4 Click OK.

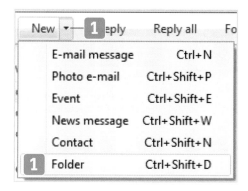

DID YOU KNOW?
Using the same technique, you can create subfolders inside folders you create.

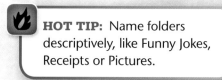
HOT TIP: Name folders descriptively, like Funny Jokes, Receipts or Pictures.

Move email to a folder

Moving an email from one folder (like your inbox) to another (like Funny Jokes) is a simple task. Just drag the email from one folder to the other.

1 Right-click the email message to move in the Message pane.

2 Hold down the mouse button while dragging the message to the new folder.

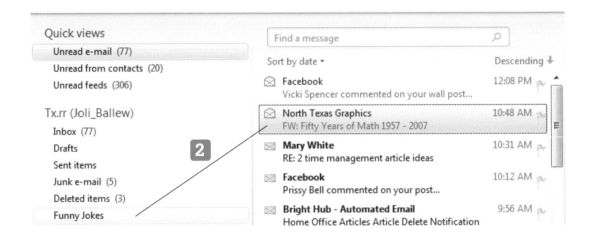

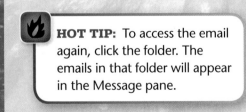
HOT TIP: To access the email again, click the folder. The emails in that folder will appear in the Message pane.

Delete email in a folder

In order to keep Mail from getting bogged down, you'll need to delete email in folders often. Depending on how much email you get, this may be as often as once a week.

1 Right-click Junk e-mail.

2 Click Empty 'Junk e-mail' folder.

3 Right-click Deleted Items.

4 Click Empty 'Deleted items' folder.

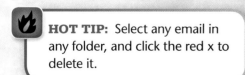

HOT TIP: Select any email in any folder, and click the red x to delete it.

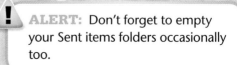

ALERT: Don't forget to empty your Sent items folders occasionally too.

10 Stay secure

Introduction

You probably know that computers can be infected by viruses, spyware or malware, and that computer users can have their credit card number or identity stolen while using the Internet. You may even know people who this has happened to or someone who has fallen for an email scam. However, if you take some precautions and use the available Windows 7 security tools properly, *you* shouldn't have anything to worry about!

Windows 7 has built-in, automatic, behind-the-scenes tools to keep you safe. If you know how to take advantage of the available safeguards, you'll be protected in almost all cases. You just need to be aware of the dangers, heed security warnings when they are given (and resolve them), and use all of the available features in Windows 7 to protect yourself and your PC.

Add a new user account

You created your user account when you first turned on your new Windows 7 PC. Your user account is what defines your personal folders as well as your settings for desktop background, screen saver and other items. You are the 'administrator' of your computer, even if your user name is Grandma or Dad. If you share the PC with someone, they should have their own user account too.

1 Click Start.

2 Click Control Panel.

3 Click Add or remove user accounts.

ALERT: If every person who accesses your PC has their own standard user account and password, and if every person logs on using that account and then logs off the PC each time they've finished using it, you'll never have to worry about anyone accessing anyone else's personal data.

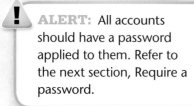

ALERT: All accounts should have a password applied to them. Refer to the next section, Require a password.

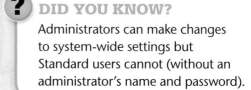

DID YOU KNOW?

Administrators can make changes to system-wide settings but Standard users cannot (without an administrator's name and password).

4 Click Create a new account.

5 Type a new account name, verify Standard user is selected, and click Create Account.

? **DID YOU KNOW?**

You can also click Change the picture, Change the account name, Remove the password and other options to further personalise the account.

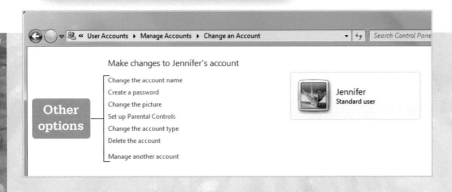

Require a password

All user accounts, even yours, should be password-protected. When a password is configured, a user must type the password to log on to your PC or laptop. This protects the PC from unauthorised access by other family members.

1 Click Start.

2 Click Control Panel.

3 Add or remove user accounts.

4 Click the user account to apply a password to.

5 Click Create Password.

6 Type the new password, type it again to confirm it and type a password hint.

7 Click Create password.

Configure Windows Update

It's very important to configure Windows Update to get and install updates automatically. This is the easiest way to ensure your computer is as up-to-date as possible, at least as far as patching security flaws Microsoft uncovers, having access to the latest features and obtaining updates to the operating system itself. I propose you verify that the recommended settings are enabled as detailed here, and occasionally check for optional updates manually.

1 Click Start.

2 Click Control Panel.

3 Click System and Security.

> **! ALERT:** After clicking System and Security, you may see that optional components or updates are available. You can view these updates and install them if desired.

WHAT DOES THIS MEAN?

Windows Update: if enabled and configured properly, when you are online, Windows 7 will check for security updates automatically and install them. You don't have to do anything, and your PC is always updated with the latest security patches and features.

4 Click Windows Update.

5 In the left pane, click Change settings.

6 Configure the settings as shown here, and click OK.

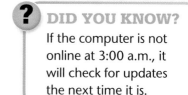

? DID YOU KNOW?

If the computer is not online at 3:00 a.m., it will check for updates the next time it is.

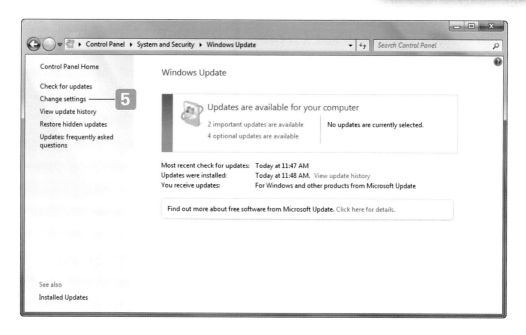

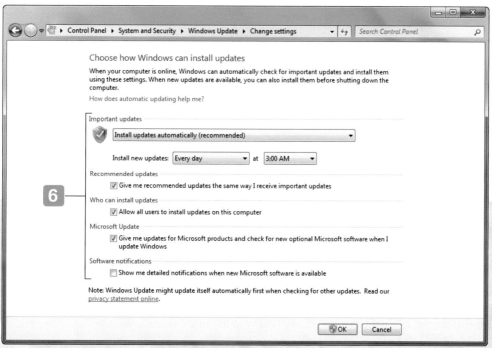

Scan for viruses with Windows Defender

You don't have to do much to Windows Defender except understand that it offers protection against Internet threats like malware. It's enabled by default and it runs in the background. However, if you ever think your computer has been attacked by an Internet threat (virus, worm, malware, etc.) you can run a manual scan here.

1 Open Windows Defender. (Click Start, type Defender, and under Control Panel click Windows Defender.)

2 Click the arrow next to Scan (not the Scan icon). Click Full scan if you think the computer has been infected.

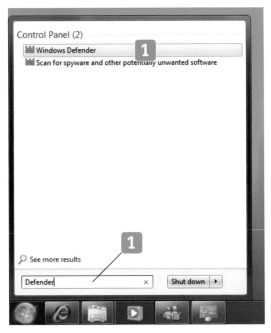

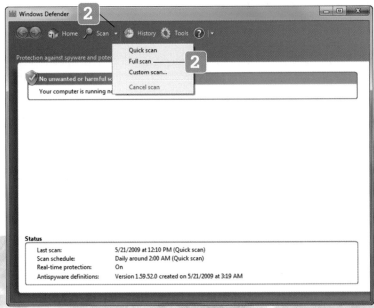

WHAT DOES THIS MEAN?

Malware: stands for malicious software. Malware includes viruses, worms, spyware, etc.

Enable the Firewall

Windows Firewall is a software program that checks the data that comes in from the Internet (or a local network) and then decides whether it's good data or bad. If it deems the data harmless, it will allow it to come through the firewall, if not, it's blocked.

1 Open Windows Firewall.

2 From the left pane, click Turn Windows Firewall on or off.

3 Verify the Firewall settings match what's shown here.

4 Click OK.

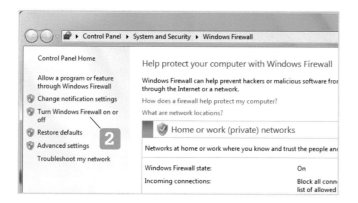

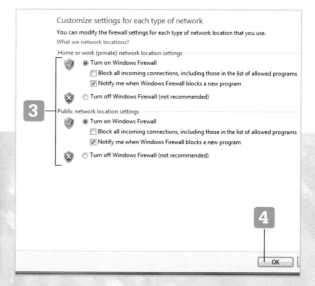

ALERT: You have to have a firewall to keep hackers from getting access to your PC, and to help prevent your computer from sending out malicious code if it is ever attacked by a virus or worm.

View and resolve Action Center warnings

Windows 7 tries hard to take care of your PC and your data. You'll see a pop-up if your anti-virus software is out of date (or not installed), if you don't have the proper security settings configured, or if Windows Update or the Firewall is disabled. You'll also get a user account control prompt each time you want to install a program or make a system-wide change.

1 Open the Action Center.

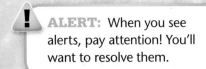 **ALERT:** When you see alerts, pay attention! You'll want to resolve them.

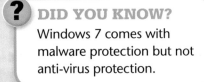 **DID YOU KNOW?**
Windows 7 comes with malware protection but not anti-virus protection.

2 If there's anything in red or yellow, read about the problem and click the option to resolve it. (Here, you'd click Find a program online, followed by Set up backup.)

3 View the resolution and perform the task.

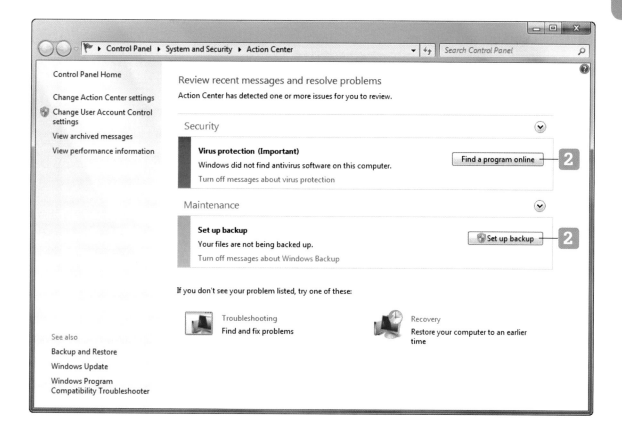

ALERT: Install anti-virus software to protect your PC from viruses and worms.

WHAT DOES THIS MEAN?

Virus: a self-replicating program that infects computers with intent to do harm. Viruses often come in the form of an attachment in an email or in a program you download from the Internet.

Worm: a self-replicating program that infects computers with intent to do harm. However, unlike a virus, it does not need to attach itself to a running program.

Create a basic backup

Windows 7 comes with a backup program you can use to back up your personal data. The backup program is called Backup and Restore.

1 Open Backup and Restore.

2 Click Set up backup. (Once it's set up, the button will change to Back up now.)

HOT TIP: Since backups can be large, consider a USB drive, external hard drive or DVD. You can also choose a network location.

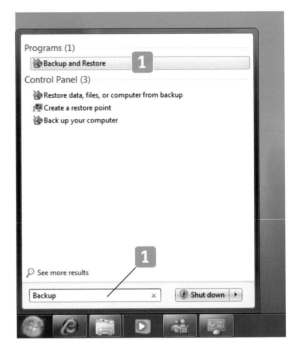

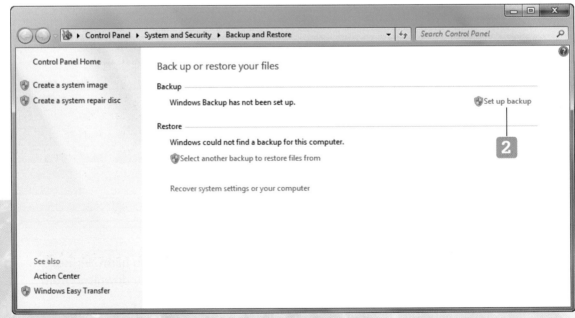

3. Choose a place to save your backup. Click Next. (If you don't have a backup device, you may want to choose Save on a network.)

4. Select Let Windows choose (recommended).

5. Wait while the backup completes.

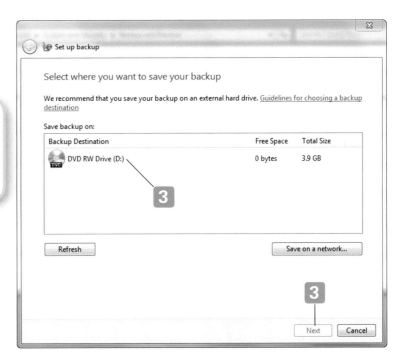

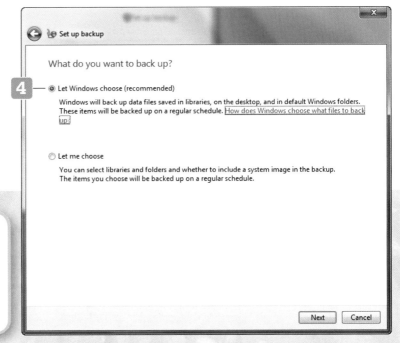

Use Disk Cleanup

Disk Cleanup won't make your PC more secure, but it is a safe and effective way to reduce unnecessary data on your PC. With unnecessary data deleted, your PC will run faster and have more available disk space for saving files and installing programs (and Windows Updates!). With Disk Cleanup you can remove temporary files, empty the Recycle Bin, remove setup log files and downloaded program files (among other things), all in a single process.

1 Open Disk Cleanup.

2 If prompted to choose a drive or partition, choose the letter of the drive that contains the operating system, which is almost always C:, but occasionally D:. Click OK.

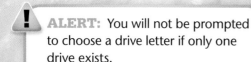

ALERT: You will not be prompted to choose a drive letter if only one drive exists.

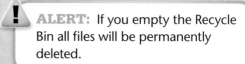

ALERT: If you empty the Recycle Bin all files will be permanently deleted.

3 Select the files to delete. Accept the defaults if you aren't sure.

4 Click OK to start the cleaning process.

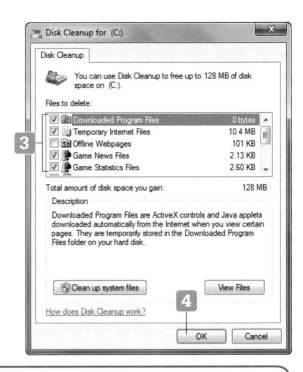

WHAT DOES THIS MEAN?

Downloaded Program Files: these are files that download automatically when you view certain webpages. They are stored temporarily in a folder on your hard disk, and accessed when and if needed.

Temporary Internet Files: these files contain copies of webpages you've visited on your hard drive, so that you can view the pages more quickly when visiting the page again.

Offline Webpages: these are webpages that you've chosen to store on your computer so you can view them without being connected to the Internet. Upon connection, the data is synchronised.

Game News Files: data acquired from the Internet regarding items in your Game Library.

Game Statistics Files: these are files related to games you've played, like how many wins and losses you have.

Hibernation File Cleaner: these files are related to information about your PC as it enters hibernation. If problems occur during hibernation, you'll want this information, otherwise, you can delete it.

Recycle Bin: the Recycle Bin contains files you've deleted. Files are not permanently deleted until you empty the Recycle Bin.

Setup Log Files: files created by Windows during set-up processes.

Temporary Files: files created and stored by programs for use by the program. Most of these temporary files are deleted when you exit the program, but some do remain.

Thumbnails: these are small icons of your pictures, videos and documents. Thumbnails will be recreated as needed, even if you delete them here.

Per user archived Windows Error Reporting: files used for error reporting and solution checking.

Use Disk Defragmenter

A hard drive stores the files and data on your computer. When you want to access a file, on a traditional PC or laptop, the hard drive spins, and data is accessed from the drive (this isn't what happens on a solid state drive). When the data required for the file you need is all in one place, the data is accessed more quickly than if it is scattered across the hard drive in different areas. When data is scattered, it's fragmented.

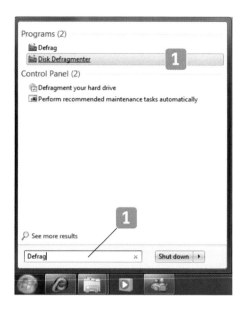

1 Open Disk Defragmenter.

2 Verify that Disk Defragmenter is configured to run on a schedule. If not, click Configure schedule.

3 To manually run Disk Defragmenter, click Defragment disk.

4 Click Close.

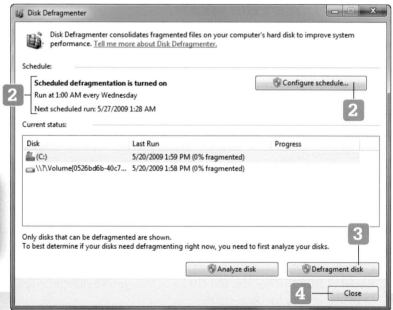

HOT TIP: You won't need to defragment your disk if it isn't fragmented!

? DID YOU KNOW?

Disk Defragmenter analyses the data stored on your hard drive and consolidates files that are not stored together.

? DID YOU KNOW?

By default, Disk Defragmenter runs automatically, and on a schedule, but it is best to verify this.

11 Working with files and folders

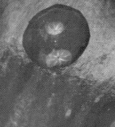

Introduction

You're going to have data to save. That data may come in the form of letters you type on the computer, pictures you take using your digital camera, music you copy from your own CD collection, email addresses, travel information, videos from a DV camera, holiday card and gift lists, and more. Each time you click the Save or Save As button under a file menu (which is what you do to save data to your PC most of the time), you'll be prompted to tell Windows 7 *where* you want to save the data. For the most part though, Windows 7 will *tell you* where it thinks you should save the data. Documents go in the Documents folder, music in the Music folder, pictures in the Pictures folder, and so on.

In this chapter you'll learn where files are saved by default, and how to create your own folders and subfolders for organising data. You'll also learn how to copy, move and delete files and folders, and how to locate saved files in various ways. You'll also learn how to create a basic backup to an external hard drive, like a USB stick.

Create a folder

Microsoft understands what types of data you want to save to your computer, and built Windows 7's folder structure based on that information. Look at the Start menu. You'll see your name at the top. Clicking your name on the Start menu opens your personal folder.

While Windows 7's default folders will suit your needs for a while, it won't last. Soon you'll need to create subfolders inside those folders to manage your data and keep it organised. You may also want to create a folder on the desktop to hold information you access often.

1 Right-click an empty area of your desktop.

2 Point to New.

3 Click Folder.

4 Type a name for the folder.

5 Press Enter on the keyboard.

ALERT: If you can't type a name for the folder, right-click the folder and select Rename.

? DID YOU KNOW?
You can drag the folder to another area of the desktop or even to another area of the hard drive to move it there.

HOT TIP: Create a folder to hold data related to a hobby, tax information, holidays or family.

Create a subfolder

You can also create folders inside other folders. For instance, inside the Documents folder, you may want to create a subfolder called Tax Information to hold scanned receipts, tax records and account information. Inside the Pictures folder you might create folders named 2010, 20011, 2012, or Weddings, Holidays, Family, and so on.

1 Click Start.

2 Click your user name to open your personal folder.

3 Click New folder.

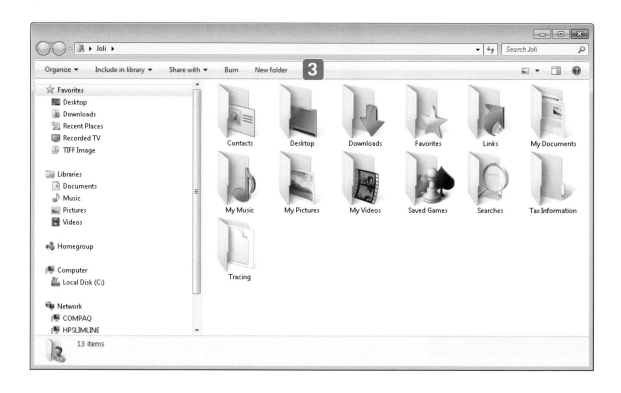

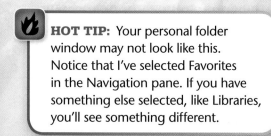

HOT TIP: Your personal folder window may not look like this. Notice that I've selected Favorites in the Navigation pane. If you have something else selected, like Libraries, you'll see something different.

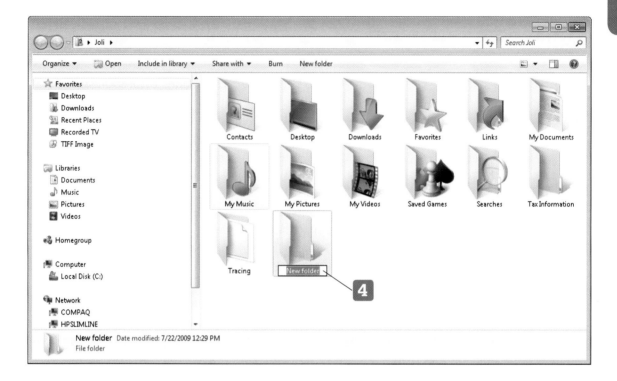

4 Type a name for the folder.

5 Press Enter on the keyboard.

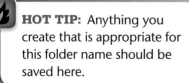

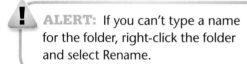

ALERT: If you can't type a name for the folder, right-click the folder and select Rename.

HOT TIP: Anything you create that is appropriate for this folder name should be saved here.

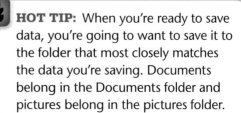

HOT TIP: When you're ready to save data, you're going to want to save it to the folder that most closely matches the data you're saving. Documents belong in the Documents folder and pictures belong in the pictures folder.

WHAT DOES THIS MEAN?

Your personal folder contains the following folders, which in turn contain data you've saved:

Contacts: this folder contains your contacts' information, which includes email addresses, pictures, phone numbers, home and business addresses, and more.

Desktop: this folder contains links to items for data you created on your desktop.

My Documents: this folder contains documents you've saved, subfolders you created and folders created by Windows 7.

Downloads: this folder does not contain anything by default. It does offer a place to save items you download from the Internet, like drivers and third-party programs.

Favorites: this folder contains the items in Internet Explorer's Favorites list. It may also include folders created by the computer manufacturer or Microsoft, including Links, Microsoft Websites and MSN Websites.

Links: this folder contains shortcuts to the Documents, Music, Pictures, Public, Recently Changed, and Searches folders.

My Music: this folder contains sample music and music you save to the PC.

My Pictures: this folder contains sample pictures and pictures you save to the PC.

Saved Games: this folder contains games that ship with Windows 7 and offers a place to save games you acquire on your own.

Searches: this folder contains preconfigured Search folders including Recent Documents, Recent Email, Recent Music, Recent Pictures and Videos, Recently Changed, and Shared By Me. If you need to find something recently accessed or changed and don't know where to look, you can probably locate it here. These folders get updated each time you open them.

My Videos: this folder contains sample videos and videos you save to the PC.

Copy a file

Folders contain files. Files can be documents, pictures, music, videos, and more. Sometimes you'll need to copy a file to another location. Perhaps you want to copy the files to an external drive, memory card or USB thumb drive for the purpose of backing them up, or maybe you want to create a copy so you can edit the data in them without worrying about changing the original. You can find files in your personal folders.

1 Locate a file to copy.

2 Right-click the file.

3 While holding down the right mouse key, drag the file to the new location.

4 Drop it there.

5 Choose Copy Here.

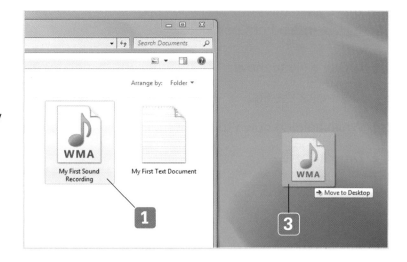

DID YOU KNOW?
In the example shown here I'm copying a file to the desktop. You can copy files to other folders using the same method, but you'll have to open the folder first.

HOT TIP: Even though the icon has Move to Desktop written under it, after you drop the file you'll have the option to move or to copy.

Move a file

When you copy something, an exact duplicate is made. The original copy of the data remains where it is, and a copy of it is placed somewhere else. For the most part, this is not what you want to do when organising data. When organising data, you generally want to move the data. If a picture of a graduation needs to be put in the Graduation Pictures folder, you need to move it, not copy it.

You move a file the same way you copy one, except when you drop the file you choose Move Here instead of Copy Here.

1 Locate a file to move. (See the previous section for more information.)

2 Right-click the file.

3 While holding down the right mouse key, drag the file to the new location.

4 Drop it there.

5 Choose Move Here.

Copy Here
Move Here —— **5**
Create Shortcuts Here
Cancel

 HOT TIP: If you don't have any files yet, you can locate a picture file in the Pictures folder. Click Start, click Pictures, and open the Sample Pictures folder (by double-clicking it).

 HOT TIP: To put the file back in its original location, repeat these steps dragging the file from the desktop back to the Sample Pictures folder.

Delete a file

When you are sure you no longer need a particular file, you can delete it. Deleting it sends the file to the Recycle Bin. This file can be 'restored' if you decide you need the file later, provided you have not emptied the Recycle Bin since deleting it.

1 Locate a file to delete.

2 Right-click the file.

3 Choose Delete.

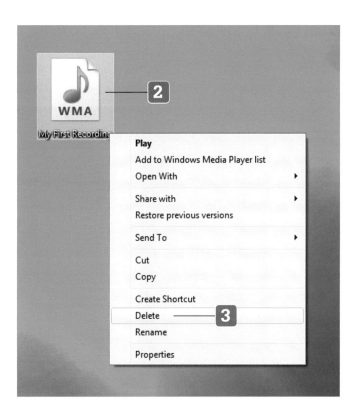

Copy a folder

Folders often contain other folders. Folders contain files including documents, pictures, music, videos, and more. Sometimes you'll need to copy a folder to another location. Perhaps you want to copy the folder to an external drive, memory card or USB thumb drive for the purpose of backing it up, or maybe you want to create a copy so you can edit the data in it without worrying about changing the original. You can find folders in your personal folders.

1 Locate a folder to copy.

2 Right-click the folder.

3 While holding down the right mouse key, drag the folder to the new location.

4 Drop it there.

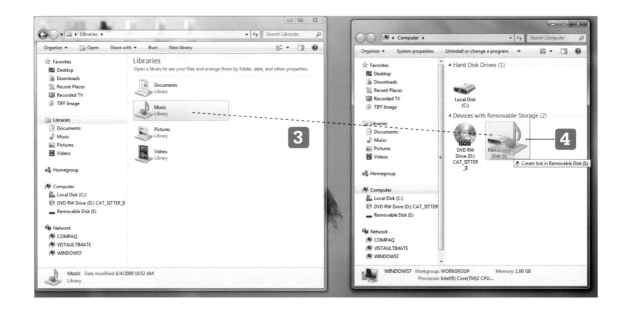

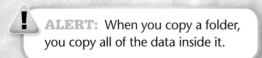

ALERT: When you copy a folder, you copy all of the data inside it.

HOT TIP: If you don't have any folders yet, you can copy the Sample Pictures folder.

5 Choose Copy Here.

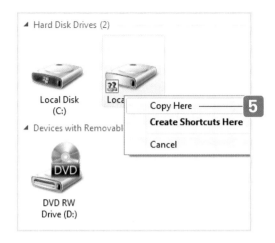

Move a folder

When you copy something, an exact duplicate is made. The original copy of the data remains where it is, and a copy of it is placed somewhere else. For the most part, this is not what you want to do when organising data. When organising data, you generally want to move the data. If you created a folder called Work on your desktop for instance, you may want to move the folder (and all its contents) to the inside of your personal folder.

You move a file the same way you copy one, except when you drop the file you choose Move Here instead of Copy Here.

1 Locate a folder to move.

2 Open the folder you want to move it to. (For instance, open your personal folder by clicking your name on the Start menu.)

3 Right-click the folder.

4 While holding down the right mouse key, drag the file to the new location.

5 Drop it there.

6 Choose Move Here.

> **? DID YOU KNOW?**
> You may have to open a folder to locate the folder you want to move.

> **HOT TIP:** I suggest you move the folder you created on your desktop earlier to your personal folder, that is, if you're working through this chapter sequentially.

> **HOT TIP:** To put the file back in its original location, repeat these steps dragging the file from the desktop back to the original location.

Delete a folder

When you are sure you no longer need a particular folder, you can delete it. When you delete a folder you delete the folder and everything in it. Deleting it sends the folder and its contents to the Recycle Bin. This folder can be 'restored' if you decide you need it later, provided you have not emptied the Recycle Bin since deleting it.

1 Locate a folder to delete.

2 Right-click the folder.

3 Choose Delete.

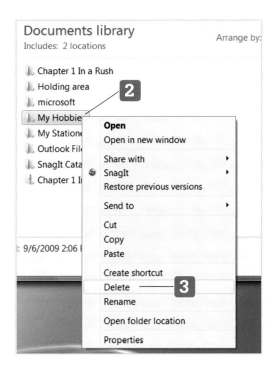

? DID YOU KNOW?

It's best to keep unwanted or unnecessary data off your hard drive. That means you should delete data you don't need, including items in the Recycle Bin.

Open a saved file

If you recall, a file can be a document, picture, song, video, presentation, database or other item. You can create documents in Notepad, upload photos from a digital camera, purchase music online and perform other tasks to obtain data. Once data (in this case, a file) is saved to your hard drive, you can access it, open it, and often modify it.

1 Click Start.

2 Click Documents.

3 Locate the file to open in the Documents folder.

4 Double-click it to open it.

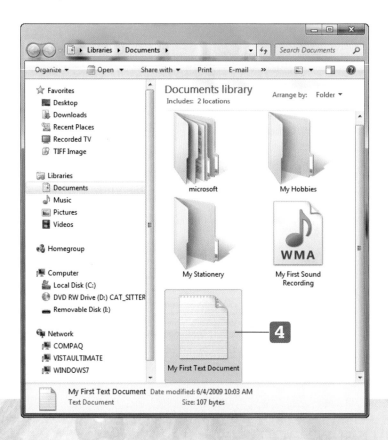

HOT TIP: Most of the time, you open a saved file from a personal folder or a folder you've created.

DID YOU KNOW?
The file will open in the appropriate program automatically.

Search for a file

After you create data, like a Notepad document, you save it to your hard drive. When you're ready to use the file again, you have to locate it and open it. There are several ways to locate a saved file. If you know the document is in the Documents folder, you can click Start, and then click Documents. Then, you can simply double-click the file to open it. However, if you aren't sure where the file is, you can search for it from the Start menu.

1 Click Start.

2 In the Start Search window, type the name of the file.

3 Click the file to open it. There will be multiple search results.

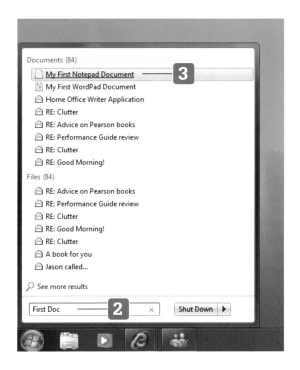

! ALERT: If you don't know the exact name of the file, you can type part of the name.

? DID YOU KNOW?
If you don't know any part of the name of the file, you can type a word that is included inside the file or a specific type of file.

Browse for a file

Sometimes you'll open a program first, and then open a file associated with it. For instance, you may open Notepad, and then open a text file using the File>Open command. After clicking Open, you'll then 'browse' for the file you want. Browsing is the process of locating a file by looking through the available folders on your hard drive from inside an open program.

1 Open Notepad.

2 Click File, and click Open.

3 Double-click the file to open. If you do not see the file, proceed to step 4.

4 In any area in the window, locate the folder that contains the document to open. Double-click the file to open it.

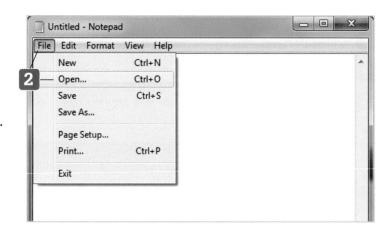

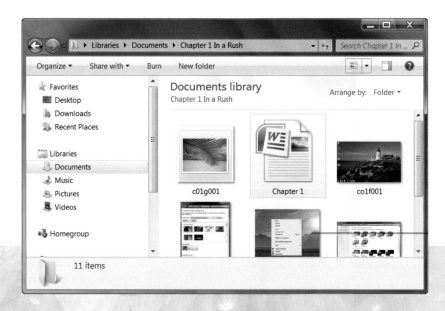

SEE ALSO: Write a letter with Notepad, and Save a letter with Notepad in Chapter 3.

? DID YOU KNOW?
You can also single-click a file and then click Open.

Explore for a file

Exploring for a file is a bit more complex than the other methods. In this method, you open Windows Explorer and use the Explorer window to locate the file to open.

1 Right-click the Start button and click Open Windows Explorer.

2 Maximise the window and resize the panes to view the contents of the window.

3 In the left pane, expand and collapse folders until you have located the file to open.

4 Double-click the file to open it.

SEE ALSO: Resize a window, Chapter 1.

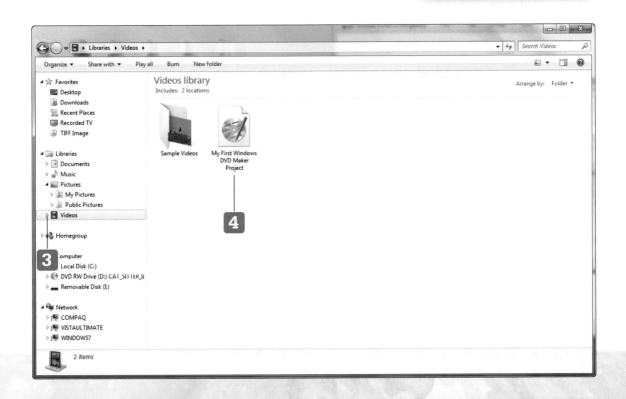

HOT TIP: You can resize the panes too, using the same technique you use to resize a window, by dragging the separator bars.

? DID YOU KNOW?
To expand and collapse any folder, click the arrow next to it.

Back up a folder to an external drive

Once you have your data saved in folders, you can copy the folders to an external drive to create a backup. You copy the folder to the external drive the same way you'd copy a folder to another area of your hard drive; you open both folders and drag and drop.

1 Click Start and click Computer. Position the window so it only takes up about half of the desktop.

2 Locate the external drive. (Leave this window open.)

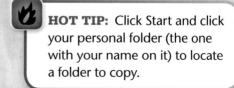

ALERT: Before you begin, plug in and/or attach the external drive.

HOT TIP: Click Start and click your personal folder (the one with your name on it) to locate a folder to copy.

3 Locate a folder to copy. If necessary position the window that contains the folder so you can see both open windows.

4 Right-click the folder to copy.

5 While holding down the right mouse key, drag the folder to the new location.

6 Drop it there and choose Copy Here.

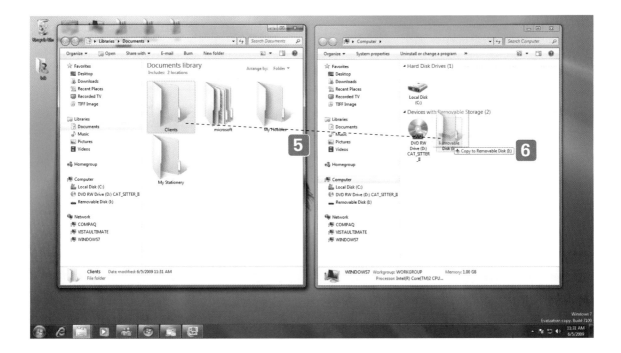

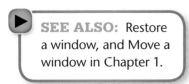
SEE ALSO: Restore a window, and Move a window in Chapter 1.

ALERT: Don't choose Move Here. This will move the folder off the computer and onto the external hard drive.

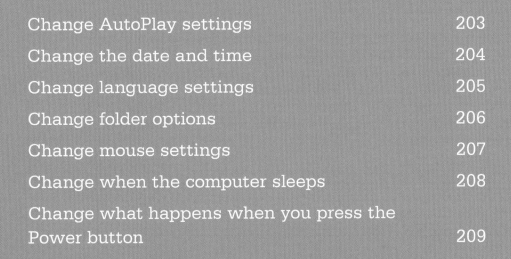

12 Change system defaults

Introduction

Windows 7 comes preconfigured with certain settings called system defaults. These include things like the mouse pointer type and speed, how much idle time should pass before the computer goes to sleep, and how folders look on the screen. You can make changes to these defaults along with other settings automatically configured, like the date and time, the language, what happens when you insert a DVD into the DVD drive, and similar items.

Change AutoPlay settings

Windows 7 makes a decision each time you insert a blank CD, a DVD movie, a picture CD or a music CD by opening the program it thinks you'll most probably want to use. Alternatively, you may be prompted each time regarding your preference. You can tell Windows 7 what you want it to do when you insert or access media though, and configure what program should be used to open what type of media (and to open it in that program automatically).

1 Click Start.

2 Click Default Programs. (It's on the Start menu.)

3 Click Change AutoPlay settings.

4 Use the drop-down lists to select the program to use for the media you want to play.

5 Click Save.

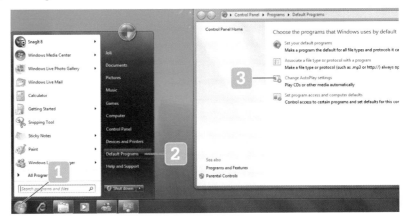

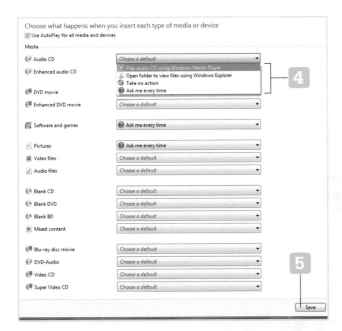

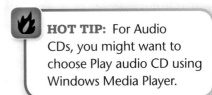

HOT TIP: For Audio CDs, you might want to choose Play audio CD using Windows Media Player.

Change the date and time

If there is ever a need to change the date and time (or the time zone), you can do so from the Date and Time dialogue box.

1 Click Start.

2 Click Control Panel.

3 Click Clock, Language, and Region.

4 Click Set the time and date.

5 Click Change date and time.

6 Use the arrows or type in a new time.

7 Select a new date.

8 Click OK.

9 Click OK.

HOT TIP: Click the Additional Clocks tab to add a second clock in a different time zone.

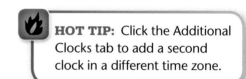

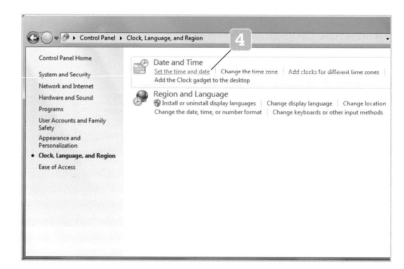

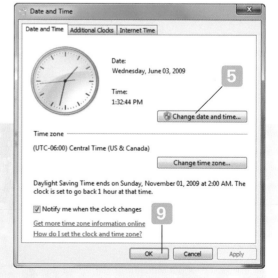

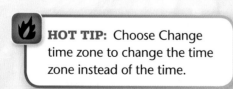

HOT TIP: Choose Change time zone to change the time zone instead of the time.

Change language settings

When you travel with a laptop computer, you may need to change the country or region, the date, time and number format. If you speak and work in multiple languages, you may also need to change keyboards or other input methods. You can do this from the Control Panel.

1 Click Start.

2 Click Control Panel.

3 Click Region and Language.

4 Work through each tab, starting with the Formats tab.

5 Make changes as desired from the available drop-down lists.

6 Click OK.

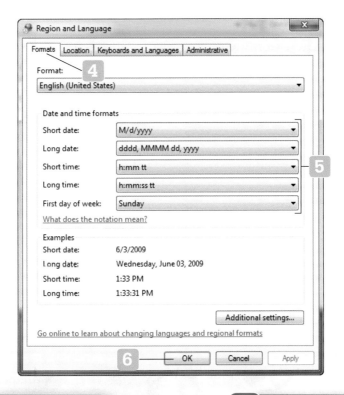

 HOT TIP: To set your current location, click the Location tab and select the desired country from the drop-down list.

Change folder options

You can change how folders look using Folder Options. You can use a single-click (instead of a double-click) to open a folder, choose to open each folder in its own window, view hidden files and folders, and more.

1 Click Start.

2 In the Start Search window, type Folder Options.

3 Under Programs in the results list, click Folder Options.

4 From the General tab, read the options and make changes as desired.

5 From the View tab, read the options and make changes as desired.

6 From the Search tab, read the options and make changes as desired.

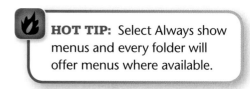

HOT TIP: Select Always show menus and every folder will offer menus where available.

HOT TIP: To shorten the list of search results, deselect Find partial matches.

Change mouse settings

The speed the mouse moves, the pointer shaper, vertical scrolling and other mouse options are all configured with default settings. You can change the settings, perhaps turning a right-handed mouse into a left-handed mouse, using Mouse settings.

1 Click Start, and in the Start Search window, type mouse.

2 In the results, under Programs, click Mouse.

3 From the Buttons tab, read the options and make changes as desired.

4 From the Pointers tab, select a theme as desired.

5 From the Pointer Options tab, read the options and make changes as desired.

6 From the Wheel tab, read the options and make changes as desired.

7 Click OK.

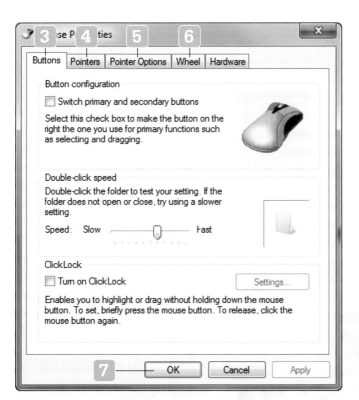

HOT TIP: If you're not happy with how fast the pointer moves when you move your mouse, you can change that speed here.

HOT TIP: Enable Snap To and the mouse will move to the default option in dialogue boxes.

Change when the computer sleeps

Your computer is configured to go to sleep after a specific period of idle time. If you do not want your computer to go to sleep, for instance if Media Center is supposed to record something in the middle of the night, you can change this behaviour.

1 Click Start, and in the Start Search window type Power.

2 In the results, under Programs, click Power Options.

3 Click Change when the computer sleeps.

4 Use the drop-down lists to make changes as desired.

5 Click Save changes.

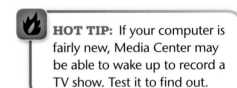

HOT TIP: If your computer is fairly new, Media Center may be able to wake up to record a TV show. Test it to find out.

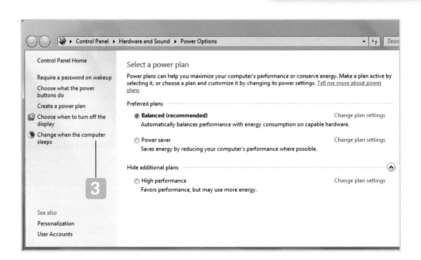

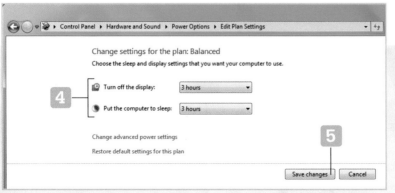

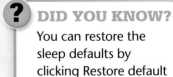

DID YOU KNOW?

You can restore the sleep defaults by clicking Restore default settings for this plan.

Change what happens when you press the Power button

Your computer is configured to do something specific when you press the Power button. By default, this is to shut down the computer but you can change this behaviour.

1 Click Start, and in the Start Search window type Power.

2 In the results, under Programs, click Power Options.

3 Click Choose what the power buttons do.

4 Use the drop-down lists to make changes as desired.

5 Click Save changes.

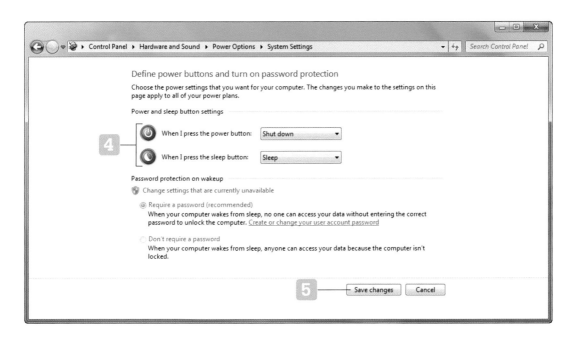

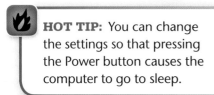

HOT TIP: You can change the settings so that pressing the Power button causes the computer to go to sleep.

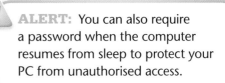

ALERT: You can also require a password when the computer resumes from sleep to protect your PC from unauthorised access.

13 Create a HomeGroup, and share data and printers

Introduction

Windows 7 lets you share data with other computers on your network. You can do this most simplistically by creating a homegroup on a private home network and having your other Windows 7 PCs join it. Once you've created a homegroup, you can share data, media, pictures and other items easily.

There are other ways to share data though; you can save or move data to the supplied Public folders for instance, or you can create shared folders manually. You can also share printers and other hardware for use by others on your network or others who use your PC.

Note: Homegroups only work to share data with other Windows 7 PCs. If you have XP or Vista PCs, you'll want to use the Public folders or create your own shared folders.

Locate the Public folders and create a desktop shortcut

You can share data with others on your network or those who share your PC from the Public folders. The Public folders are located on your local disk, generally C, under Users, and in Public.

1 Click Start.

2 Click Computer.

3 Double-click Local Disk C (or whatever letter represents your hard drive).

4 Double-click Users.

5 Right-click Public, click Send to, and click Desktop (create shortcut).

6 Close the Computer window.

◢ Hard Disk Drives (1)

Local Disk (C:) — **3**

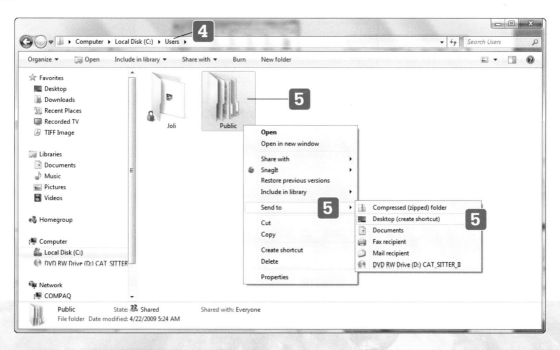

HOT TIP: If you share a computer, save the data you want to share in Public folders for easy access by other users.

HOT TIP: Any time you want to share data with others on your network, move or copy it to these folders.

Create a HomeGroup

You can share data in many ways using varying techniques. However, using a HomeGroup enables sharing by the easiest method. You create a HomeGroup in the Network and Sharing Center.

1 Open the Network and Sharing Center. (Click Start, in the Start Search window type Network and Sharing, and click Network and Sharing Center.)

2 Click Ready to Create, by HomeGroup.

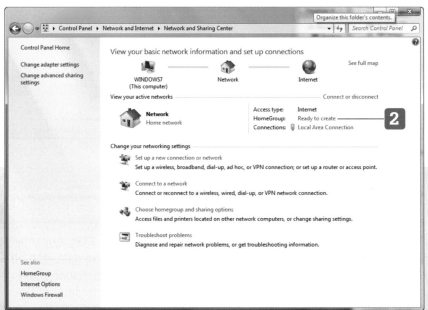

3 Click Create a homegroup.

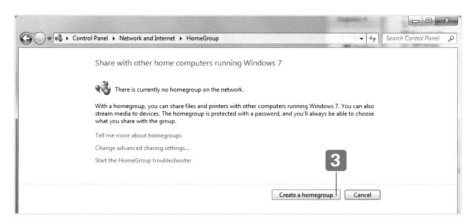

4 Choose what you want to share, and click Next.

5 Write down the password; you'll need it to have other Windows 7 PCs join the HomeGroup. Click Finish.

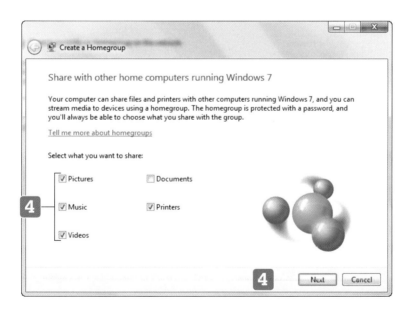

ALERT: Computers must be running Windows 7 to participate in the HomeGroup. If you have other computers on your network that aren't running Windows 7, you'll want to share data using the Public folders, detailed in this chapter.

HOT TIP: If you ever forget the password, simply open Network and Sharing Center, click Choose homegroup and sharing options, and click View or print the HomeGroup password.

Save data to the Public folder

To share data with anyone on your network or anyone who can also access your PC, save the data to share in the Public folders.

1 Open a picture, document or other item you wish to save to the Public folders.

2 Click File, and click Save As.

3 In the Save As dialogue box, in the left pane, click Desktop. You'll then be able to double-click the Public shortcut you created earlier.

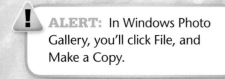
ALERT: In Windows Photo Gallery, you'll click File, and Make a Copy.

HOT TIP: Save pictures to the Public Pictures folder. Save documents to the Public Documents folder.

4 Select the Public subfolder to save to.

5 Type a name for the file.

6 Click Save.

 HOT TIP: The Public folders contain built-in subfolders like Public Documents, Public Downloads and Public Pictures.

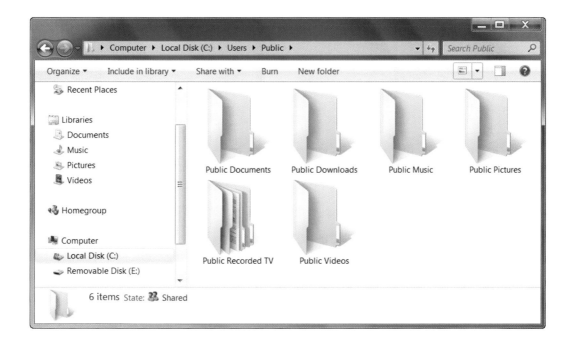

 **DID YOU KNOW?**
It's actually better to move data you want to share into the Public folders. That way, you won't create duplicate copies of the data on your hard drive.

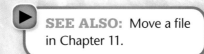 **SEE ALSO:** Move a file in Chapter 11.

Copy or move data to the Public folder

You can access the Public folder by browsing to it. This may require you to browse the network if the Public folders are stored on another PC. However, if you put a shortcut to the Public folder on your desktop as detailed earlier in this chapter, you only need to double-click the folder to open it.

Once you have access to the Public folder you can drag items to the folder for sharing. As detailed in Chapter 5, it's best to right-click the data while dragging. That way, you can decide if you want to copy the data or move it.

1 Open the Public folder.

2 Locate the data you want to copy or move. You may have to position the two windows as shown here.

3 Choose Copy Here, Move Here, or Create Shortcuts Here, as desired.

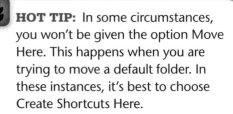

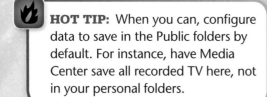
HOT TIP: When you can, configure data to save in the Public folders by default. For instance, have Media Center save all recorded TV here, not in your personal folders.

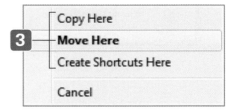
HOT TIP: In some circumstances, you won't be given the option Move Here. This happens when you are trying to move a default folder. In these instances, it's best to choose Create Shortcuts Here.

Share a personal folder

Sometimes you won't want to move or copy data into Public folders and subfolders. Instead, you'll want to share data directly from your own personal folders. To do this, you'll have to manually share the desired personal folders yourself.

1 Locate the folder to share.

2 Right-click the folder.

3 Choose Share with, and click Homegroup.

4 Choose Read to give users permission to view the files; choose Read/Write if you want users to be able to change the files too. Remember though, a homegroup can be joined only by other Windows 7 PCs. If you want to share with specific people who are not in a homegroup, choose Specific people.

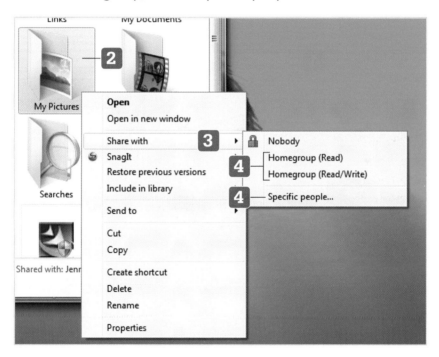

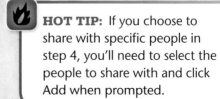

HOT TIP: You can apply advanced sharing options in the Network and Sharing Center, by clicking Choose homegroup and sharing options.

HOT TIP: If you choose to share with specific people in step 4, you'll need to select the people to share with and click Add when prompted.

View a shared printer and/or add a printer

When you create a homegroup, printer sharing is automatically enabled. You can view shared printers from the Devices and Printers window in Windows 7 PCs. You can also add a printer that's connected to another PC from the Devices and Printers window. If you are not in a homegroup, you'll need to share your printers and devices manually.

1 Click Start, and in the Start Search window, type Printers.

2 Under Control Panel, click View devices and printers.

3 Locate the shared printers. They will have a green tick beside them.

4 To add a printer, click Add a printer.

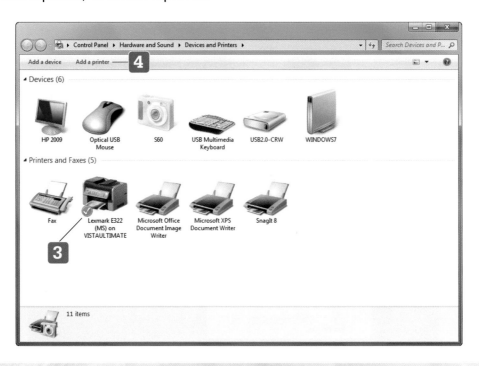

5 Locate the printer to add in the list and click Next.

6 Continue to follow the prompts, as needed.

HOT TIP: Right-click any printer to see its properties, what's printing, and more.

ALERT: When others on your network access the printer for the first time, they may be prompted to install a driver for it. This is OK and will be managed by the PC.

14 Fix problems

Introduction

When problems arise, you will want to resolve them quickly. Windows 7 offers plenty of help. System Restore can fix problems automatically by 'restoring' your computer to an earlier time. If the boot-up process is slow, you can disable unwanted start-up items with the System Configuration tool. Additionally, you can use the Network and Sharing Center to help you resolve connectivity problems and use Device Manager to 'roll back' a driver that didn't work, and if your computer seems bogged down you can delete unwanted programs and files easily.

Use System Restore

System Restore regularly creates and saves *restore points* that contain information about your computer that Windows uses to work properly. If your computer starts acting oddly, you can use System Restore to restore your computer to a time when the computer was working properly.

1 Open System Restore.

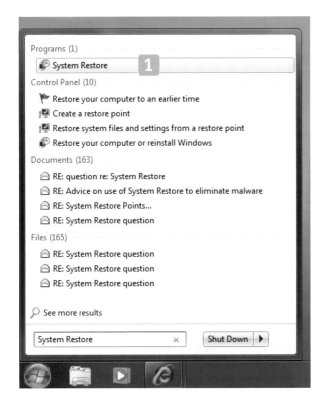

? DID YOU KNOW?

Because System Restore works only with its own system files, running System Restore will not affect any of your personal data. Your pictures, email, documents, music, etc. will not be deleted or changed.

WHAT DOES THIS MEAN?

Restore point: a snapshot of the Registry and system state that can be used to make an unstable computer stable again.

Registry: a part of the operating system that contains information about hardware configuration and settings, user configuration and preferences, software configuration and preferences, and other system-specific information.

2 Click Next to accept and apply the recommended restore point.

3 Click Finish.

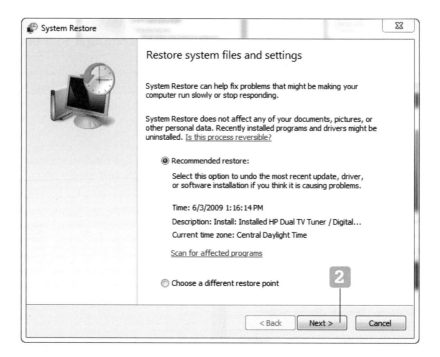

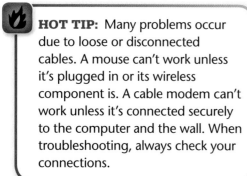

HOT TIP: Many problems occur due to loose or disconnected cables. A mouse can't work unless it's plugged in or its wireless component is. A cable modem can't work unless it's connected securely to the computer and the wall. When troubleshooting, always check your connections.

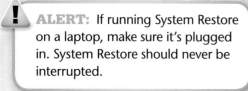

ALERT: If running System Restore on a laptop, make sure it's plugged in. System Restore should never be interrupted.

Disable unwanted start-up items

Lots of programs and applications start when you boot up your computer. This causes the start-up process to take longer than it should, and programs that start also run in the background, slowing down computer performance. You should disable unwanted start-up items to improve all-round performance.

ALERT: Do not deselect anything you don't recognise, or the operating system!

1 Click Start.

2 In the Start Search window, type system configuration.

3 Under Programs, click System Configuration.

4 From the Startup tab, deselect third-party programs you recognise but do not use daily.

5 Click OK.

HOT TIP: If you see a long list under the System Configuration's Startup tab, go through it carefully and consider uninstalling unwanted programs from Control Panel.

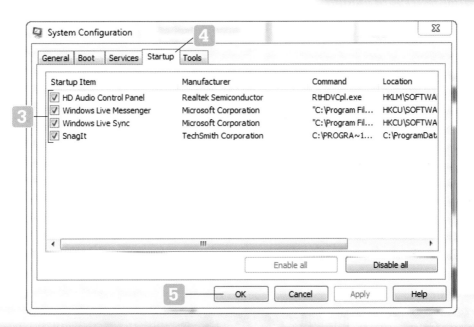

DID YOU KNOW?
Even if you disable a program from starting when Windows does, you can start it when you need it by clicking it in the Start and All Programs menu.

ALERT: You'll have to restart the computer to apply the changes.

Resolve Internet connectivity problems

When you have a problem connecting to your local network or to the Internet, you can often resolve the problem in the Network and Sharing Center.

1 Open the Network and Sharing Center.

2 Click the red X.

3 Perform the steps in the order they are presented.

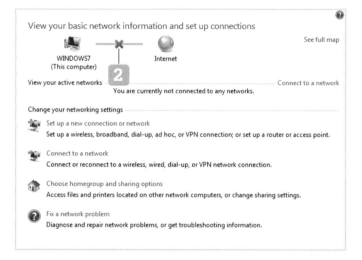

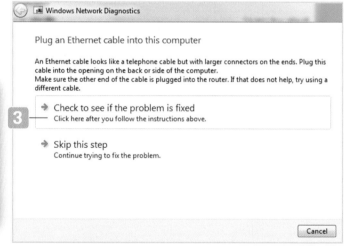

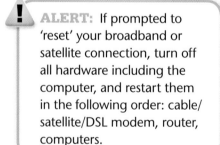

ALERT: If prompted to 'reset' your broadband or satellite connection, turn off all hardware including the computer, and restart them in the following order: cable/ satellite/DSL modem, router, computers.

? DID YOU KNOW?
Almost all of the time, performing the first step will resolve your network problem.

! ALERT: When restarting a cable or satellite modem, remove any batteries to turn off the modem completely.

Use Device Driver Rollback

If you download and install a new driver for a piece of hardware and it doesn't work properly, you can use Device Driver Rollback to return to the previously installed driver.

1 Click Start.

2 Right-click Computer.

3 Click Properties.

4 Under Tasks, click Device Manager (not shown).

5 Click the triangle next to the hardware that uses the driver to rollback. It will change to a minus sign.

6 Double-click the device name.

7 Click the Driver tab and click Roll Back Driver.

8 Click OK.

ALERT: The Roll Back Driver option will only be available if a new driver has recently been installed.

DID YOU KNOW?
Many hardware items have multiple connections and connection types. If one type of connection doesn't work, like USB, try FireWire.

ALERT: You can only rollback to the previous driver. This means that if you have a driver (D) and then install a new driver (D1) and it doesn't work, and then you install another driver (D2) and it doesn't work, using Device Driver Rollback will revert to D1, *not* the driver (D) before it.

View available hard drive space

Problems can occur when hard drive space gets too low. This can become a problem when you use a computer to record television shows or movies (these require a lot of hard drive space) or if your hard drive is partitioned.

1 Click Start.

2 Click Computer.

3 In the Computer window, right-click the C drive and choose Properties.

4 View the available space.

ALERT: If you find you are low on disk space, you'll have to delete unnecessary files and/or applications.

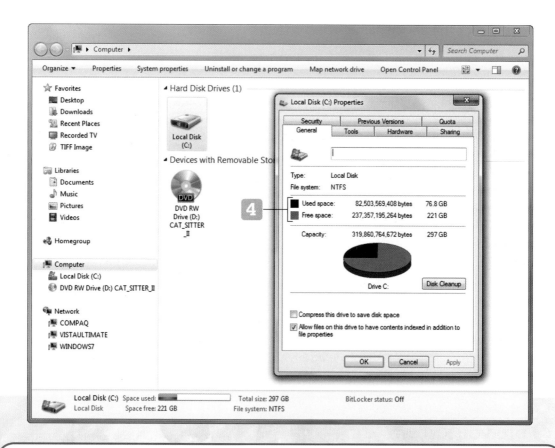

WHAT DOES THIS MEAN?

Partition: some hard drives are configured to have multiple sections, called partitions. The C: partition may have 20 GB available, while the D: partition may have 60 GB. If you save everything to the C: partition (failing to use the D: partition), it can get full quickly.

Delete unwanted Media Center media

One of the places you'll find data that hogs disk space is in Media Center's storage areas. This is especially true if you record television programmes or movies, or create your own movies. TV and movies take up a lot of hard drive space.

1 Open Media Center.

2 Under TV + Movies, click recorded tv.

3 Right-click any recording and click Delete.

4 Repeat as necessary.

recorded tv

 DID YOU KNOW?
You can also find unwanted media in the Video and Pictures libraries.

 HOT TIP: If you see that a series is recording that you don't watch, right-click, choose Series Info, and click Cancel Series.

Uninstall unwanted programs

If you haven't used an application in more than a year, you probably never will. You can uninstall unwanted programs from the Control Panel.

1 Click Start, click Control Panel.

2 In Control Panel, click Uninstall a program.

3 Scroll through the list. Click a program name if you want to uninstall it.

4 Click Uninstall.

5 Follow the prompts to uninstall the program.

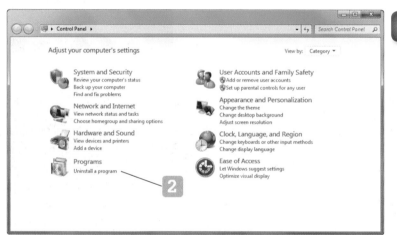

HOT TIP: Look for programs in the list that start with the name of the manufacturer of your computer (Acer, Hewlett-Packard, Dell, etc.).

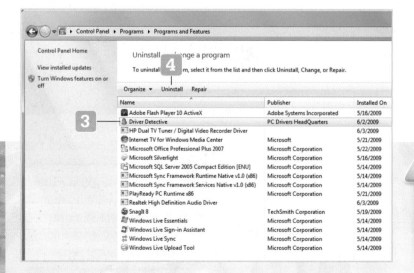

ALERT: Your computer may have come with programs you don't even know about. Perform these steps to find out.

Top 10 Windows 7 Problems Solved

Problem 1: I can't find Windows Mail or Windows Photo Gallery!

You have to download and install these two programs now; they're not included with Windows 7 by default. There are only a few steps. Go to the website, click the Download link, and wait for the download and installation process to complete.

1 Open Internet Explorer and go to http://www.windowslive.com/.

2 Look for the Download now button and click it. You'll be prompted to click Download now once more on the next screen.

3 Click Run, and when prompted, click Yes.

4 When prompted, select the items to download. If the programs have already been installed by the computer manufacturer, you'll be informed what programs were installed and what is still available.

5 When prompted to select your settings, make the desired choices. You can't go wrong here; there are no bad options.

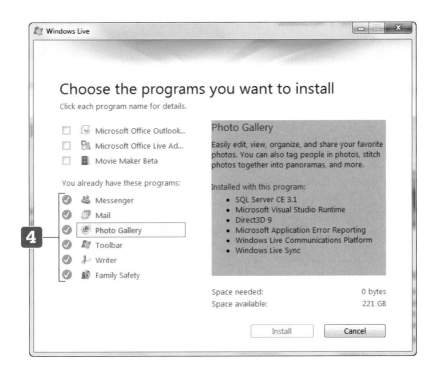

Windows Live

Choose the programs you want to install
Click each program name for details.

- ☐ Microsoft Office Outlook...
- ☐ Microsoft Office Live Ad...
- ☐ Movie Maker Beta

You already have these programs:

- ✓ Messenger
- ✓ Mail
- ✓ Photo Gallery
- ✓ Toolbar
- ✓ Writer
- ✓ Family Safety

Photo Gallery

Easily edit, view, organize, and share your favorite photos. You can also tag people in photos, stitch photos together into panoramas, and more.

Installed with this program:

- SQL Server CE 3.1
- Microsoft Visual Studio Runtime
- Direct3D 9
- Microsoft Application Error Reporting
- Windows Live Communications Platform
- Windows Live Sync

| Space needed: | 0 bytes |
| Space available: | 221 GB |

Install   Cancel

? DID YOU KNOW?

It's OK to select all of these programs if you think you'll use them; they are all free. However, Family Safety can get a tad annoying, so only install that if you have children who will use your computer.

Problem 2: I lost my Internet connection

If you are having trouble connecting to the Internet, you can diagnose Internet problems using the Network and Sharing Center. However, if you have just installed new hardware, it is probably best to call your ISP for help first.

1 Open the Network and Sharing Center.

2 To diagnose a nonworking Internet connection, click the red x.

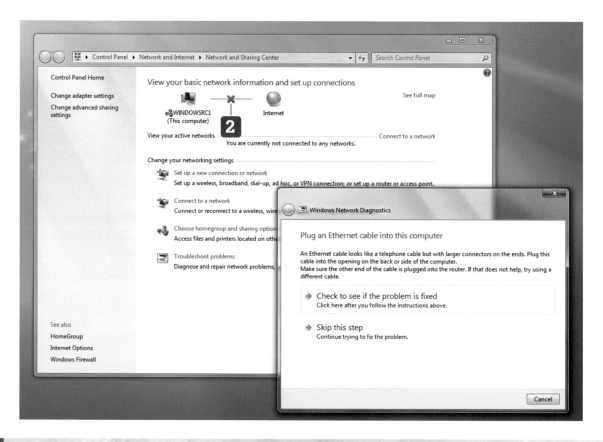

ALERT: If you are connected to the Internet, you will see a green line between your computer and the Internet. If you are not connected you will see a red x.

3 Take the suggested steps to resolve the problem. Note the troubleshooter here says the problem is indeed resolved after plugging in the Ethernet cable.

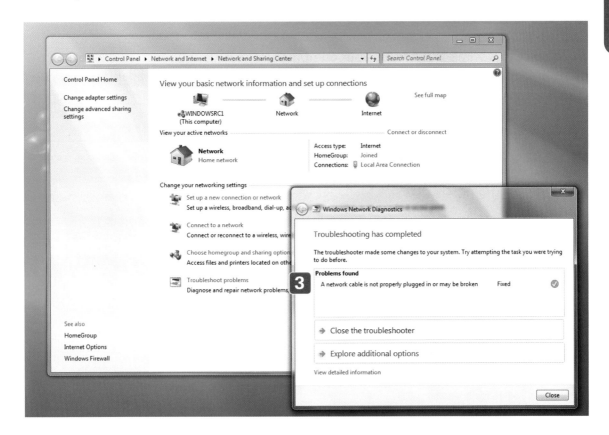

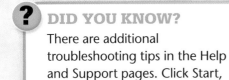

Problem 3: I can't connect to a wireless network

To connect to a wireless network, your computer must have the required wireless hardware. Specifically, you need a built-in wireless card (or a wireless adapter). You can find out if you have this hardware using Device Manager.

1 Click Start.

2 In the Start Search dialogue box, type Device Manager.

3 Under Programs, click Device Manager to open it.

4 Locate Network adapters. (Wireless hardware is called network adapters.)

5 Click the plus sign to expand it: it will then become a minus sign.

6 Look for a device with the word 'wireless' in it. If you do not see a wireless adapter listed, you do not have wireless capabilities.

7 Click the X in the top right corner of Device Manager to close it.

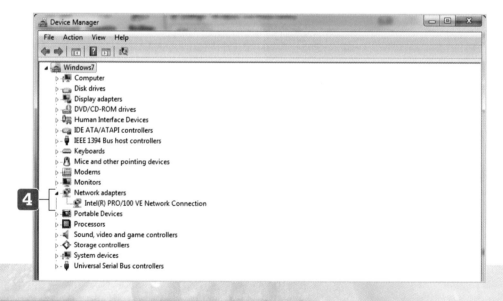

? DID YOU KNOW?

Even if you have no adapters, you can purchase a USB converter to obtain satellite Internet or a modem to use dial-up. There's always a way to get online!

Problem 4: The text on webpages is too small for me to read

If your over 50s eyes give you trouble reading what's on a webpage because the text is too small, use the Page Zoom feature. Page Zoom works by preserving the fundamental design of the webpage you're viewing. This means that Page Zoom intelligently zooms in on the entire page, which maintains the page's integrity, layout, and look.

1 Open Internet Explorer and browse to a webpage.

2 Click the arrow located at the bottom right of Internet Explorer to show the Zoom options.

3 Click 150%.

4 Notice how the webpage text and images increase. Use the scroll bars to navigate the page.

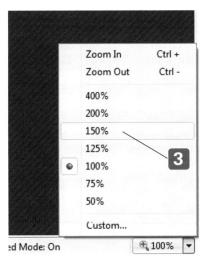

Problem 5: I think I might have a virus

Windows 7 does not come with anti-virus software, so if you haven't done so already, you should purchase and install this kind of software. You can try AVG free or purchase software from Norton or McAfee. Windows Defender does offer protection against Internet threats like malware though. It's enabled by default and it runs in the background. If you ever think your computer has been attacked by an Internet threat (virus, worm, malware, etc.) you can run a manual scan here.

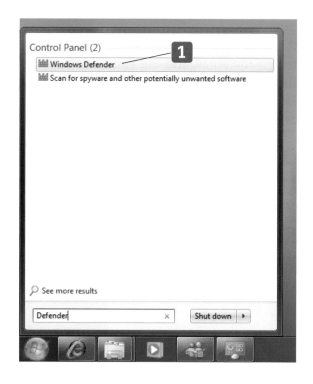

1. Open Windows Defender. (Click Start, type Defender, and under Control Panel click Windows Defender.)

2. Click the arrow next to Scan (not the Scan icon). Click Full scan if you think the computer has been infected.

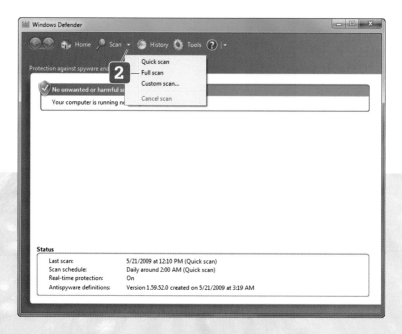

Problem 6: I keep seeing warnings that there's something wrong with my computer

Windows 7 tries hard to take care of your PC and your data. You'll see a pop-up if your anti-virus software is out of date (or not installed), if you don't have the proper security settings configured, or if Windows Update or the Firewall is disabled. You'll also get a user account control prompt each time you want to install a program or make a system-wide change.

1 Open the Action Center.

2 If there's anything in red or yellow, read about the problem and click the option to resolve it. (Here, you'd click Find a program online, followed by Set up backup.)

3 View the resolution and perform the task.

ALERT: When you see alerts, pay attention! You'll want to resolve them.

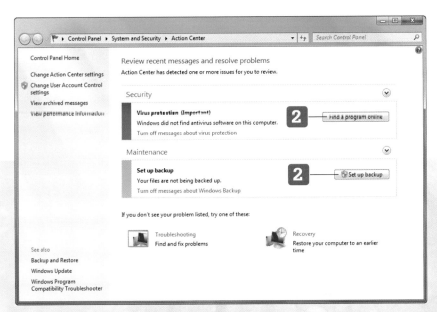

Problem 7: How do I back up my data?

Windows 7 comes with a backup program you can use to back up your personal data. The backup program is called Backup and Restore.

1 Open Backup and Restore.

2 Click Set up backup. (Once it's set up, the button will change to Back up now.)

HOT TIP: Since backups can be large, consider a USB drive, external hard drive or DVD. You can also choose a network location.

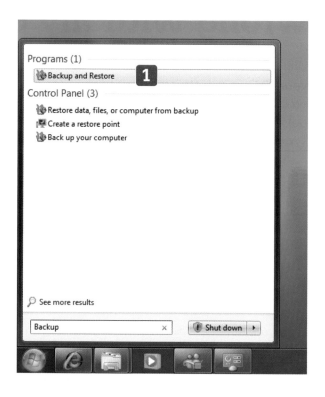

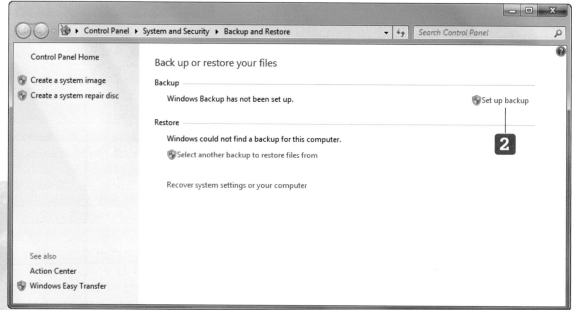

3 Choose a place to save your backup. Click Next. (If you don't have a backup device, you may want to choose Save on a network.)

4 Select Let Windows choose (recommended).

5 Wait while the backup completes.

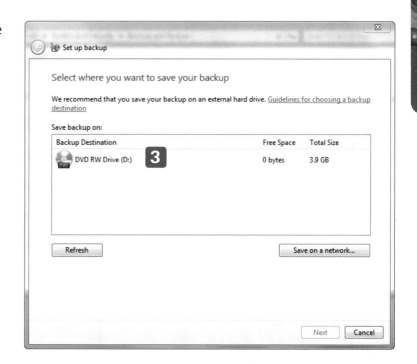

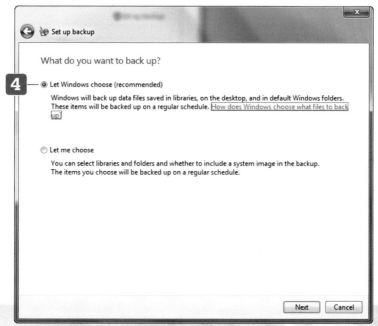

? DID YOU KNOW?

You can't create a backup on the hard disk of the computer you are backing up.

? DID YOU KNOW?

You may be prompted to insert a blank DVD, or insert a USB drive depending on the choice made in step 3.

Problem 8: My computer is running slowly

Disk Cleanup is a safe and effective way to reduce unnecessary data on your PC. With unnecessary data deleted, your PC will run faster and have more available disk space for saving files and installing programs. With Disk Cleanup you can remove temporary files, empty the Recycle Bin, remove setup log files and downloaded program files (among other things), all in a single process.

1 Open Disk Cleanup.

2 If prompted to choose a drive or partition, choose the letter of the drive that contains the operating system, which is almost always C, but occasionally D. Click OK.

3 Select the files to delete. Accept the defaults if you aren't sure.

4 Click OK to start the cleaning process.

! ALERT: You may not be prompted to choose a drive letter if only one drive exists.

! ALERT: If you empty the Recycle Bin all files will be permanently deleted.

Problem 9: I want something specific to happen when I insert a CD or a DVD

Windows 7 makes a decision each time you insert a blank CD, a DVD movie, a picture CD or a music CD by opening the program it thinks you'll most probably want to use. Alternatively, you may be prompted each time regarding your preference. You can tell Windows 7 what you want it to do when you insert or access media though, and configure what program should be used to open what type of media (and to open it in that program automatically).

1 Click Start.

2 Click Default Programs. (It's on the Start menu.)

3 Click Change AutoPlay settings.

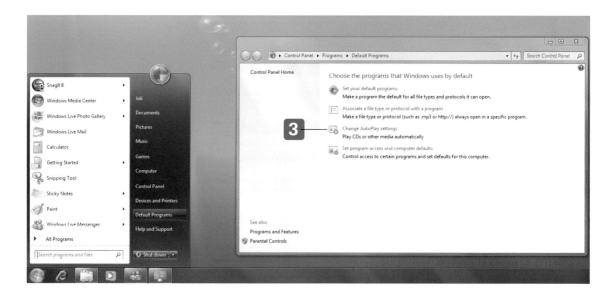

4 Use the drop-down lists to select the program to use for the media you want to play.

5 Click Save.

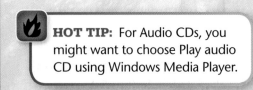

HOT TIP: For Audio CDs, you might want to choose Play audio CD using Windows Media Player.

Problem 10: I can't watch live TV in Media Center

To watch live TV, you have to tell Media Center how you connect to your TV signal (and your PC has to have a TV tuner). There are many ways to watch TV, including but not limited to using an antenna, using a cable box, making a connection directly from a coaxial connection in the wall, using a satellite dish, and more.

1 Use the arrow keys on the keyboard or remote control to locate TV and live tv setup.

2 Choose the options that apply to your TV setup and connection. You may have to input a zip code (postcode), choose what type of connection you use, agree to some terms of service, and/or answer other questions regarding your TV service.

3 As prompted, make the proper choices, working through the wizard. Click Finish when done.

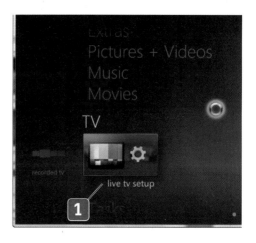

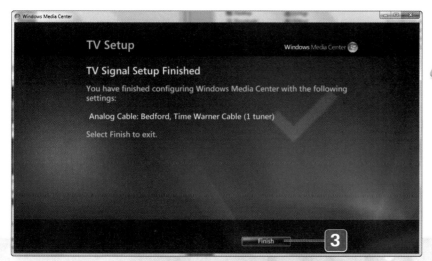

ALERT: Make sure you're connected to the Internet during the set-up process so that the Guide can download the latest information.

ALERT: If you get a message when working through this that no TV tuner is installed, you'll have to purchase an external TV tuner.

HOT TIP: Once the signal is set up, Windows Media Center will download information for up to 14 days of TV programming. You can use the results to record and watch television.

USE YOUR COMPUTER WITH CONFIDENCE

9780273723547

9780273723509

9780273723486

9780273723479

9780273723523

9780273723493

9780273723554

In Simple Steps guides guarantee immediate results. They teach you exactly what you want and need to know on any application; from the most essential tasks to master through to solving the most common problems you'll encounter.

- **<u>Practical</u>** – explains and provides practical solutions to the most commonly encountered problems

- **<u>Easy to understand</u>** – jargon and technical terms explained in simple English

- **<u>Visual</u>** – full colour large screen shots

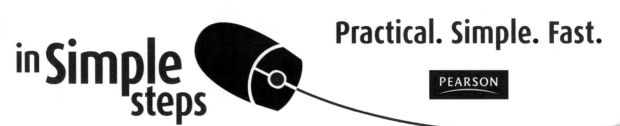

Practical. Simple. Fast.

PEARSON